JOHN DONNE
and his world

DEREK PARKER

JOHN DONNE

and his world

THAMES AND HUDSON

LONDON

Frontispiece: Donne in the pose of a
melancholy lover; portrait by an
unknown artist *c.* 1595, when the
poet was in his early twenties.

Printed in Great Britain by
Jarrold and Sons Ltd, Norwich

THE ROMANTIC, apparently contradictory life of John Donne makes it easy to think of him as a theatrical figure, one moment the lover, the next the ascetic; first the man of action, then the theologian; once the headstrong wooer, at last the preaching skeleton, descending from the pulpit after his last sermon to pose for the standing statue of himself in his shroud – the most impressive *memento mori* of them all.

Yet in fact his life is all of a piece: in one of his last sermons he compares the kiss of Judas with the kiss of a woman – 'About midnight [Jesus] was taken and bound with a kiss. Art thou not too conformable to him in that? Is not that too literally, too exactly, thy case? At midnight to have been taken and bound with a kiss?' His poems addressed to God are as much poems of love as the early verses he so much wanted to suppress. In his end is his beginning.

We do not know precisely when that beginning was. Donne was born in London, sometime between January and June 1572 – in the fourteenth year of the reign of Queen Elizabeth I. On his mother's side both the literary and religious strains of his character were represented: she was the youngest daughter of John Heywood, a singer and musician, and the author and producer of 'interludes' or short dramas performed at court and in colleges and Inns of Court – plays such as the *Pyramus and Thisbe* performed by Bottom and his friends in Shakespeare's *A Midsummer Night's Dream*. But Heywood was also the

London in the sixteenth century. Bread Street, where Donne lived as a child, runs northward from the river, just to the right of the centre of the map.

5

husband of a niece of the great Sir Thomas More, beheaded for constancy to his religion less than forty years before Donne's birth. Here was not only a tradition of literature and intellectuality (More had been a friend of Erasmus), but of suffering in the cause of religion. Donne was, as he was to write in his *Pseudo-Martyr* (1610), 'derived from such a stock and race as I believe no family ... hath endured and suffered more in their persons and fortunes, for obeying the teachers of Roman doctrine, than it hath done.'

His father's lineage is less interesting, though he believed it to be distinguished. He thought himself descended from an ancient family, Dwn of Kidwelly, in Wales, one of whose members had borne a sword at the coronation of King Arthur. More recently, it was certainly true that the Donnes had served with Glendower against Henry IV, had supported the Yorkists during the Wars of the Roses, and that a John Donne had been knighted by Edward IV after the Battle of Tewkesbury, and had died in 1503. That branch of the family had recently become extinct, but Donne counted himself of its blood. His own father was, less nobly, an ironmonger, his name entered in the roll of the Ironmongers' Company in 1556–57.

By the time his eldest son was born, he was in a good way of trade, frequently in attendance on the Lord Mayor of London, a torch-bearer in processions, and perhaps a sharp man of business, for in 1570 he was summoned (and not for the first time) for failing to record, officially, seven tons of coal he had bought. He fell out, too, with his father-in-law, driven abroad after the accession of Elizabeth (he had been a favourite at Queen Mary's Court). Heywood complained that his son-in-law had pocketed the profits of a lease which had been left in his care, and 'not one penny of it paid or sent hither unto me for my maintenance'.

(Opposite) John Heywood, Donne's maternal grandfather.

(*Above*) The Lord Mayor of London moves in procession through his city: Donne's father often preceded him on such occasions.

(*Opposite*) Broadsheets kept the people in mind of Popish plots and treasons: of which the Armada and the alleged attempt to poison Queen Elizabeth were but two

John Donne senior died after only twelve years of marriage – he was in his early forties, his wife over ten years younger, and left with six surviving children: Elizabeth, Anne, John, Henry, Mary and Katherine. Her husband left about £3500. There has always been argument about the value of the pound in sixteenth-century England, relative to its value in the twentieth century, and recent inflation has further confused the matter. As a very rough guide, it might be fair to suggest that £1 in the final years of the sixteenth century would be worth between £25 and £30 today. Donne's father's fortune would have amounted to the equivalent, then, of at least £87,000. Even if there is argument about the amount, there was certainly enough to ensure his family's immediate comfort. But in any event, six months after his death, Elizabeth Donne remarried. Her second husband was a fifty-year-old doctor, John Syminges, trained in Oxford and Italy, and distinguished enough to have been several times President of the Royal College of Physicians. He was a widower with two married daughters, and evidently quite happy to care for the Donne children, though by the time they left their old home in Bread Street, in 1583, to move to a house nearer St Bartholomew's Hospital, the two youngest girls had died (Elizabeth, the eldest, was to live only for a few more years).

Syminges had probably been a friend of the Donne family for some time, for he was, like them, of 'the old religion'. Catholics were drawn together, towards the end of Elizabeth's reign, by the breaking-down of the more tolerant attitude towards them which had been allowed earlier in the age. Fierce persecutions were again possible. There was, for instance, a vicious fine of £20 a month on Roman

OXONIVM nobile Angliæ oppidum, Septentrionalem Tamesis ripam elegantissimo atque salubri situ illustrat.

Depingeb. Georg. Hoef:

Oxford, where (according to William Harison) students 'ruffle and roist it out, exceeding in apparel and haunting riotous company which draweth them from their books'. A good room at Oxford or Cambridge in the sixteenth century cost from 10s. to £1 a year.

Catholic recusants, who refused to go to church with the Protestants on Sundays and Holy Days; Catholic priests were liable to death for high treason. By now many Catholics were living in France, some at college in Douai or elsewhere training as missionaries. By the time King James came to the throne in 1603, there were over five hundred priests working secretly in England.

When the time came for Syminges to engage a tutor for his eldest stepson, he found a good Catholic – Donne makes this clear in *Pseudo-Martyr*. The extent to which his education was Jesuitical has been disputed, but he was well aware of the secret comings and goings of the missionary priests from the Continent – including his uncle, Jasper Heywood, who came to London when Donne was nine, and two years later was captured, imprisoned, and tried for high treason (though he escaped the flames). That event, and the trials of other priests, had their effect upon the impressionable boy:

Sir Henry Wotton, who in his youth became a friend of Donne, and remained so until the latter's death.

'I had my first breeding and conversation with men of suppressed and afflicted religion, accustomed to the despite of death and hungry of an imagined martyrdom. . . .'

Though life for a Catholic in Elizabethan England was difficult and could be dangerous, it was possible to adhere to one's own religion if one was cautious and unflamboyant about it. When Donne and his brother Henry were sent to university at Oxford (aged twelve and eleven respectively), it was to Hart Hall that they went, where the Principal 'in his heart was a Papist', and where there were many Catholics. Life there must have been pleasant; though the under-graduates were indeed still only boys, almost children, they were intelligent boys, and Donne made at least one friend who was to last a lifetime – Henry Wotton. Oxford was made more agreeable for him by the presence there of two young cousins and an aunt, a Mrs Dawson, who kept the Blue Boar Inn.

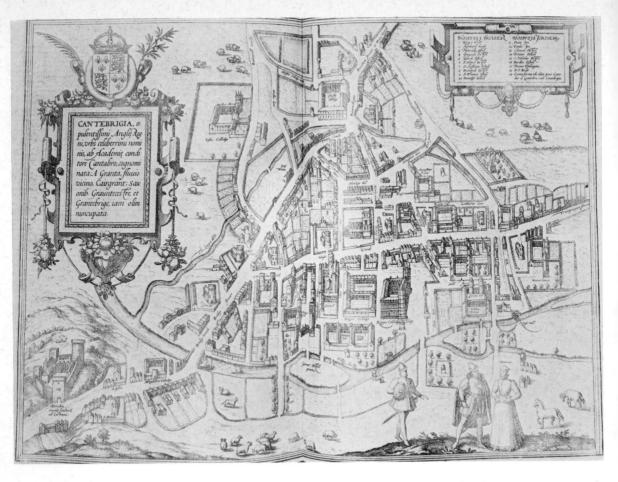

Cambridge, where, Izaak Walton says, Donne was 'a most laborious student, often changing his studies'.

Izaak Walton, who wrote the earliest life of Donne at Wotton's suggestion, says that the boy spent three years at Oxford. He left without a degree – intentionally, for undergraduates taking a degree were forced also to take the Oath of Supremacy, acknowledging the Queen as a supreme authority over the Church, and also accepting the Thirty-Nine Articles promulgated by the Church of England in 1571. No Catholic was prepared to do this.

Walton says that Donne went directly from Oxford to Cambridge, though not to a college there (for fear of running up against the same religious difficulties). Cambridge had at that time more literary associations than Oxford; Greene, Marlowe, Nashe had all recently been there, and such works as Marlowe's translations of Ovid were fresh in the libraries. Donne read deep, and discussed the new writing with his new friends. His informal studies sharpened his wit, while his training in rhetoric (a bachelor's degree then depended on skill in argument) was to serve him well in later years, when he was to become the greatest preacher of his generation. Much time at university was spent in the study of disputation, the usefulness of which some critics disputed. Lord Herbert of Cherbury wrote a generation later: 'Tutors commonly spend much time in teaching [undergraduates] subtleties of logic which, as it is usually practised, enables them for little more than to be excellent wranglers, which art, though it may be tolerable in a mercenary lawyer, I can by no means commend in a sober and well-governed gentleman.' Nevertheless, the general education was admirable, with modern history and philosophy, French and Italian, science and mathematics taking their place with the gentlemanly arts of dancing and riding.

By the time Donne left Cambridge, he must have been at least seventeen; and at this most impressionable age, we lose sight of him for two years. He probably did not spend them at home, for things there were in an uncertain state. Dr Syminges had died in 1588, and Donne's mother had moved across the Thames to the parish of St Saviour's (where she drew attention to her recusancy by refusing to go to communion). Within two years, she had married for the third time, to one Richard Rainsford. Donne may not have felt like intruding.

But where, then, did he go? Some biographers have sent him abroad on the 'grand tour', and indeed it was not uncommon for young Englishmen of the time to travel abroad to further their education. The necessary licence was easily obtained, and packet-boats sailed regularly from Dover to Calais, from Harwich to Holland, from Falmouth to Spain. Five shillings would get one to the Continent in a few hours, and while there were dangers, it was possible in an emergency to get help from a representative of England: there were Residents at Venice and Turin, Madrid and Brussels, in normal times,

'Travel in the younger sort is a part of education', wrote Francis Bacon. Over unmade roads, favoured young men travelled widely abroad in large but furiously uncomfortable coaches.

and sometimes in Constantinople and Rome. Travel was quite expensive: an income of £1000 per annum would take one in reasonable comfort about Europe for nine months or a year.

Donne would not have travelled, probably, in that kind of style, and there is no evidence that he applied for a licence. It is possible that he may have travelled, at first, as a soldier: the handsome engraving which appeared as a prefatory portrait to his *Poems* (1633), based perhaps on a lost painting by the great miniaturist Nicholas Hilliard, and done in 1591, depicts him with his right hand firmly clasping a sword. So perhaps the two conjectures have some substance. A clue is provided by an epigram, *Fall of a Wall*, which seems to refer to the siege of Corunna by an expedition of Sir Francis Drake and Sir John Norreys in 1589. This could have been written, of course, when Donne simply heard the tale of how

> *Under an undermined, and shot-bruised wall*
> *A too-brave captain perished by the fall . . .*

but it is at least possible that he was on the 1589 expedition; and if so, he could have progressed (as Walton suggests) through France and the Low Countries to Italy, and in particular to Naples to visit his Uncle Jasper, who had been deported from England on his release from the Tower in 1585, and was to die in exile.

Whatever his adventures, we hear of him next in England, as a law student: he entered Lincoln's Inn in May 1592, there to 'toughly chew, and sturdily digest Th'immense vast volumes of our common law'. Later he was to feel that he had wasted the three or four years he spent there, but this was not entirely true. For one thing, he made several good friends, with some of whom he remained in touch until the end of his life – Christopher Brooke and his brother Samuel, Rowland Woodward and his brother Thomas. He also came into contact for the first time with the Court; such of his contemporaries as Thomas and John Egerton (sons of Elizabeth's Lord Keeper) had easy access there, and he too was seen in Whitehall. Then there was the strong literary bias of Lincoln's Inn, Gray's Inn, and the Temple: Sir John Harrington, Sir John Davies, Thomas Lodge and John Marston displayed their wit at the Revels produced at the Inns, and infected Donne with the prevailing fashion for epigram, satire and social criticism.

It was at this period that he was regularly devoting time to writing, in both poetry and prose – stretching his wings as a writer. Sometimes the wing-span was not great: the *Paradoxes* and *Problems* which survive are more interesting than rewarding, but the *Elegies* and some of the love poems which may also have been written during these years, are a different matter. Donne was transmuting the urges of sex, the powerful erotic surges which he recognized as so important a part of his

(*Opposite*) Lincoln's Inn. About 150 members, with perhaps forty students, made the Inns of Court centres of cultural activity in Donne's time. The rooms were tiny, and partitioned to make them smaller: *. . . in this standing wooden chest, | Consorted with these few books, let me lie | In prison, and here be coffined, when I die.*

14

Madame

Here, where by all all Saints invoked are,
T'were too much Scisme to bee singulare,
And gainst a practise generall to warr;
yett turninge to Saints, should my Humilitee
To other Saint, then yow directed bee,
That were to make my Scisme Heresie.
nor would I bee a Convertite so cold
As not to tell yu; If thys bee to bold,
Pardons are in thys markett cheaply sold.

where because Fayth ys in too lowe degree,
I thought yt some Apostleship in mee
To speak thimgs wch by Fayth alone I see:
That ys, of yow, who are a firmament
Of vertues, where no one ys growen, nor spent,
Thay' are yor Materialls, not yor Ornament.

Others, whom wee call vertuous, are not so
In theyr whole Substance but theyr vertues grow
But in theyr Humors, and at Seasons show.

For when through tastles flatt Humilitee
In Doe-bakd men some Harmelesnes wee see
Tis but hys flegme that's vertuous and not hee.
So ys the Blood sometymes, who euer ran
To Danger unimportund, hee was than
no better then a Sanguine vertuous man.

To Cloystrall Men who in pretence of feare,
All Contributions to thys Lyfe forbear,
Haue vertu in Melancholy, and onely there.

Spirituall Cholerique Critiqs, wch in all
Religions find faults, and forgiue no fall
Haue through thys Zeale, vertu, but in theyr Gall.

we' are thus but parcell-gilt; To Gold we' are growen,
when vertu ys our Soules Complexione;
who knowes hys vertues Name, or place, hath none.

vertu ys but Aguishe when tis seuerall;
By' Occasion wakd, and Circumstantiall;
True vertu ys Soule, allways in all deeds all.

Thys vertu, thinkinge to giue Dignitee
To yor Soule found there no infirmitee;
for yor Soule was as good vertu as shee.

shee therfore wrought upon that part of yow
wch ys in scarce incredible lesse then Soule as shee could doe,
And soe hath made yor Beauty vertue to;

Foxes and goats, all beasts change when they please, | Shall women, more hot, wily, wild than these, | Be bound to one man . . . ?

personality, into these erotic poems of his youth; later the same forces were to power the almost erotically intense sermons of his middle and old age.

As with Shakespeare, so with Donne: we know nothing about the dark ladies of his youth. But that there were dark ladies is almost beyond question. There is evidence enough both in poetry and prose, though it is certainly circumstantial. In *Women's Constancy* and *The Indifferent* he specifically celebrates sexual profligacy, and justifies it in *Confined Love* and *Change*. In his *Satires* he makes it clear that he knows plenty of men who

> *. . . in rank itchy lust, desire and love*
> *The nakedness and barrenness to enjoy*
> *Of thy plump muddy whore, or prostitute boy*

and he may have been among them. He even invites women, in one of his *Paradoxes*, to enjoy as many lovers as they feel inclined: for 'what reason is there to clog any woman with one man, be he never so singular? Women had rather, and it is far better and more judicial, to enjoy all the virtues in several men, than but some of them in one – for otherwise they lose their taste, like divers sorts of meat minced together in one dish. . . .' And in another, he celebrates the proposition that 'the gifts of the body are better than those of the mind', and is thoroughly aware how beauty can suddenly swamp a man's body as with a fever: 'it strikes us suddenly, and possesseth us immoderately'.

The *Elegies* were sufficiently frank, even sufficiently scabrous, to make it impossible to print them as late as 1633, when *The Bracelet*, *On his Mistress*, *To his mistress going to bed* and *Love's Progress* were refused a licence; *Love's War* did not appear until as late as 1802:

(Opposite) The first page of a verse letter to Lady Carey and Mistress Essex Rich, written in 1612.

Here let me war; in these arms let me lie;
Here let me parley, batter, bleed, and die.
Thine arms imprison me, and mine arms thee,
Thy heart thy ransom is; take mine for me.
Other men war that they their rest may gain;
But we will rest that we may fight again.
Those wars the ignorant, these th'experienced love,
There we are always under, here above.
There engines far off breed a just true fear,
Near thrusts, pikes, stabs, yea bullets hurt not here.
There lies are wrongs; here safe uprightly lie;
There men kill men, we'will make one by and by. . . .

The pawky, quick humour, witty double-talk of such poems show Donne at his liveliest; apart from their sensuality, they are *fun* – no wonder that for two centuries and more their closeness to reality, to the humour and sheer enjoyment of sexuality, made them unacceptable; that Francis Palgrave, compiling his *Golden Treasury* in 1801, included not one poem of Donne's, repelled on the one hand by their 'indecency', on the other by their metrical roughness and inventiveness.

It is somewhat surprising that John Marriott, the publisher, was permitted to include some of the poems he did print after Donne's death in *Poems* (1633): *Tutelage*, for instance, in which the poet advances the proposition that the celebration of coitus is equivalent to a true realization of the essence of good and evil, and presents himself, the lover, as a creator who has made of his mistress 'a blissful paradise' in which her 'graces and good words' are the creatures, and on whom he has 'planted knowledge and life's tree'. *The Comparison* has passages which are obscene even to a modern reader, while nothing could be clearer than the poet's argument for downright open sexuality in *Change*: beasts pass from one lust to another – is it to be expected that women, 'more hot, wily, wild than these', should be bound to one man?

To live in one land, is captivity,
To run all countries, a wild roguery;
Waters stink soon, if in one place they bide,
And in the vast sea are worse putrified:
But when they kiss one bank, and leaving this
Never look back, but the next bank do kiss,
Then are they purest; change is the nursery
Of music, joy, life and eternity.

It is arguable that a man could write the *Elegies* without necessarily being a libertine. No doubt they could be written by someone sexually inexperienced. But they certainly could not have been written by

ANNO DNI. 1591·
ÆTATIS SVÆ·18·
ANTES MVDADO
MVERTO QVE

Donne in 1591, engraved by William Marshall perhaps after a lost original by the great Nicholas Hilliard: *a hand, or eye | By Hilliard drawn, is worth an history | By a worse painter made. . . .* The engraving is the earliest portrait of Donne known to survive, and forms the frontispiece to *Poems*, 1635.

someone lacking in sexual drive, and the (one must admit rather unpleasant) contempt for the ugly or plain man or woman, no less than their celebration of the poet's own sexual abilities, does not suggest that Donne was living a life of abstinence.

The engraving of Donne in his late teens reflects the charm celebrated by Izaak Walton in his description of the poet as an elderly man: 'of stature moderately tall; of a straight and equally-proportioned body, to which all his words and actions gave an unexpressible addition of comeliness. The melancholy and pleasant humour were in him so contempered, that each gave advantage to the other, and made his company one of the delights of mankind.' And, one might guess, of womenkind, for his contemporary Sir Richard Baker described Donne during his years at the Inns, as 'a great visitor of ladies', and he was by now spending as much of his time in love or in lust as any other young man of his age. In one of his verse-letters to a friend, 'I.L.', he grumbles because his mistress has been carried off to the north country; a sonnet to Christopher Brooke complains that he badly misses the company of his friend, and of 'the saint of his affection'.

One can sense already the beginning of a resolution of the twin aspects of his sensual life: on the one hand that overwhelming enjoyment of sexual love which makes his celebrations of the flesh so notably erotic, and on the other the spiritual power of a love centred on one woman, which was to make his love for his wife so lasting and compulsive. His sensual adventurings ('O my America! my new found land!') were giving way to a quest for a love which could embrace both sex and the spiritual. In 1617, just after his wife's death, he spoke in a sermon of the love of God which made it possible 'to exercise that same affection piously and religiously, which had before so sinfully transported and possessed it. So will a voluptuous man who is turned to God find plenty and deliciousness enough in Him to feed his soul.'

It was a cry of need. All his life, Donne sought ways of transmuting his sexuality into spirituality, and the extent to which he succeeded can be endlessly debated. In a later sermon, he reminded his congregation of the example of King Solomon, 'whose disposition was amorous and excessive in the love of women', but who 'when he turned to God departed not utterly from his old phrase and language, but having put a new and a spiritual tincture and form and habit in all his thoughts and words, conveys all his loving approaches and applications to God, and all God's gracious answers to his amorous soul into songs and Epithalamions and . . . marriages between God and his Church and between God and his soul'. It is an autobiographical statement, and moreover would have been recognized as such by listeners – even if to our ears it has somewhat the ring of an excuse (as when, for years, Victorian divines attempted to persuade readers of the Bible that the Song of Solomon was in fact a hymn of 'the mutual love of Christ and his Church'.)

Ben Jonson said that Donne had 'written all his best pieces ere he was 25 years old . . .' and it seems to be true that all the *Elegies* at least date from his time at the Inns of Court. It is remarkable how soon he was able to shake off the imitative, artificial style of the early verseletters and sonnets, and become his real self in the magnificent erotic poems of this period, which still rest on a peak of their own in the *genre*. In them, too, can be seen the grimmer Donne whose poetry and prose were to have such a keen, dark edge later in his life: in the *Epithalamion* written for a wedding, or perhaps a mockwedding, at Lincoln's Inn sometime between 1592 and 1594, while there are images of erotic delight and of simple keen pleasure, the bride is nevertheless prompted to leave a bed 'like to a grave', and the gates of the Temple open into a 'lean and hungerstarved womb' which is to be the tomb of the married couple. In the final verse the groom approaches the bride as she lies 'like an appointed lamb', to disembowel her. Even if the poem was written as a joke, for a pretendceremony, and in it Donne was attacking the made marriages of the time, the joke is a grim one.

From the 1590s too date the *Satires*, with their sharp criticism of contemporary society: the first formal satires in English, based on those of Juvenal and Horace. Harsh and rasping, they are uncomfortable works, as they were meant to be. In the first satire Donne pillories foppish lovers, 'great visitors of ladies' such as he himself was, in one guise. In the second, he turns his pen on 'poor disarm'd Papists, not worth hate', on poets, men of the theatre, libertines and petty crooks. The third speculates on the possibility of truth residing in the beliefs of various religious sects, concluding that they are all more or less contemptible – an interesting indication of Donne's own increasing susceptibility to doubt. Finally, in the fourth, he turns to the Court and the proud, lustful, bankrupt, vain, witless, false men who dwell about it; and in the fifth to the law, bitterly attacking its weakness, its slowness, its injustices, and going so far as to accuse the Queen herself of ignorance of its workings.

The *Paradoxes*, somewhat later, attack much the same targets: the fop, 'so glistering and so painted in many colours that he is hardly discerned from one of the pictures in the arras, hanging his body like an iron-bound chest, girt in and thick ribbed with broad gold laces'; the foolhardy gallant; the women, fickle, painted, cunning as vixen, malicious as serpents . . .

Donne was nothing if not critical, and cast a keen eye on lawyers and their ways. Later, too, in his sermons (especially those at Lincoln's Inn) he occasionally made jokes against them – as when, quoting St Paul on men who go to law, 'If any man will sue thee at law for thy coat, let him have thy cloak too,' he added with only the slightest pause, 'for if thy adversary have it not, thine advocate will.'

He must certainly have enjoyed his time at the Inn, for all sorts of reasons: but it was not without strain, and perhaps the most worrying (and sad) event of the period was the death of his brother Henry, who was a student at Thavies Inn. In the spring of 1593, a young Catholic priest was discovered hiding in Henry Donne's rooms, and both were thrown into prison. Under examination, perhaps under torture or threat of it, Henry Donne confessed that William Harrington was a priest, and the latter was sent for trial. By the time he was hanged, drawn and quartered, Henry Donne was also dead, of the plague, in Newgate Prison.

Apart from the natural concern he must have felt on his brother's behalf, the incident must have brought home to Donne the difficulties of his own position: no Catholic could hope to make a really successful career for himself – indeed, he would be lucky to make a career of any sort; the fact that his brother had been driven to his death (albeit in the circumstances perhaps a merciful one) by his religion

(*Opposite, above*) The Queen. 'Most fair, most dear, and most excellent Sovereign, The two windows of your Privy Chamber shall be the poles of my sphere, where, as long as Your Majesty will please to have me, I am fixed and immoveable.'

The Earl of Essex, servant and flatterer of Elizabeth I.

placed a further strain on his Catholic convictions, which in any event were never fanatical.

But if he did pause to consider theological barriers to his advancement, it was not for long. As a result of his brother's death, he received a larger proportion of his father's estate than he might otherwise have done: about £750 in all. He could now afford a boy to act as page in his rooms, and a measure of financial independence encouraged distractions from his law studies (not that he ever seems to have been inordinately enthusiastic about them). He had an 'immoderate desire of human learning', which took him to the work of poets and historians, to the play (Marlowe and Shakespeare were popular dramatists of the time), rather than to the careful study of law books. He felt free, too, to search for the kind of adventure he may have tasted on the Corunna expedition of 1589; and fortuitously, a great armada was now in preparation to sail again for Spain.

The Earl of Essex, a great national hero, was to lead the expeditionary force, and as soon as the news was out, all the youth of England

was on fire. Henry Wotton was now one of Essex's secretaries, and it was probably through him that Donne was able to get a place on one of the Queen's ships in the fleet soon to set sail from Plymouth (the ships belonging to the Navy, as opposed to those privately hired, carried the cream of the young aristocrats enlisted in the floating army: 'such gentlemen as go voluntarily, and the Commanders take note of', as a contemporary put it).

Donne always seems to have enjoyed sea travel, and images of the sea and ships appear in poems and sermons. His famous personal seal, showing Christ crucified on an anchor, has its significance.

Donne's motives for enlisting under Essex were little different from the motives of any young man going off to war in a patriotic but romantic frame of mind. In one of his *Elegies*, impossible to date but likely to have been written at about this time, he leaves his portrait with a mistress, and warns her that when he returns he may present a very different figure: white haired, his hands torn by tugging at the oars of some foreign galley, his body 'a sack of bones' burned by the sun and

Donne's famous seal which he had made in 1615 to symbolize his new career in the Church.

23

Sir Walter Raleigh, sea-adventurer, pirate, patriot, poet. 'He studied most in his sea-voyages, where he carried always a trunk of books along with him, and had nothing to divert him.'

stained by gunpowder flashes. But his patriotism was as real as his romantic longing for heroic adventure. Soon, he joined three hundred equally enthusiastic, equally inexperienced young Achilles at Plymouth; and on 3 June 1596 the fleet sailed for Cadiz.

Thirteen days later, the English ships pressed the Spanish fleet back into the inner harbour, and there Raleigh, from the *Warspite*, bombarded the Spanish flagship *San Felipe* until she ran aground and took fire. Donne watched as soldiers 'so thick as if coals had been poured out of a sack' (as Walter Raleigh put it in his report) tumbled from the ship to drown or stick fast in the mud, some burned almost to death, some grievously wounded. 'If any man had a desire to see Hell itself, it was there most lively figured', wrote Raleigh, an experienced and hardened soldier. To a young recruit, who at the most may have seen some skirmishes at Corunna, the effect must have been awful. Donne noted the end of the affair in an epigram: 'They in the sea being burnt, they in the burnt ship drowned.'

That same afternoon Sir John Wingfield led eight hundred men into the city where, wounded and unable to walk, he rode on a captured horse into the plaza to be shot through the head at the moment when the battle was won. Surely Donne, whether or not he took part in the battle itself, must have been in the Cathedral five days later when Wingfield was buried with full honours, 'the Generals throwing their handkerchiefs wet from their eyes into the grave', as an eyewitness wrote. Donne recorded the occasion in another epigram, seeing the dead commander's monument as a pillar set up by Essex to commemorate the fact that 'Farther than Wingfield no man dares to go.'

He returned to England, and as far as we know to his law studies, the wiser for having seen the unromantic face of war. The only certain fact one can put forward is that he continued to write, for the fourth of his *Satires* – and the best of them – can be dated securely at this time. The power of his intellect increases, and his technique begins to match it. But he was not to spend very long in the study, whether concentrating on his books or his poetry, for Essex was again preparing an expedition – with Raleigh as Rear-Admiral – and Donne once more enlisted. This time (the historian Stow records) there were

The Battle of Cadiz. At the moment of victory, Essex threw his hat into the sea for joy, and Raleigh ordered a fanfare of trumpets.

over five hundred 'Knights and Gentlemen voluntaries . . . bravely furnished of all things necessary (besides superfluitie in gold lace, plumes of Feathers, and such like).' The plan was to follow up the Cadiz action with another, conclusive blow against Spain by wiping out the remains of the Spanish fleet, which had been dispersed by a storm and was sheltering in Ferrol. Perhaps at the same time it would be possible to intercept at the Azores the treasure fleet sailing homeward from the West Indies.

The fleet assembled once again at Plymouth, in July 1597. After a boring wait for a fair wind, at last one came ('fresh and sweet/As to a stomach starved, whose insides meet Meat', Donne wrote) and the hundred ships sailed. Before the end of the week, they staggered back into harbour, buffeted and bruised by a violent storm which had actually sprung some of the timbers of Essex's flagship. At Falmouth, Fowey, Plymouth, many young gentlemen weak from seasickness, their gold lace tarnished and their plumes bedraggled, slid quietly ashore and vanished. Donne wrote the first of his verse-letters, to his friend Christopher Brooke, describing the storm: the noise that drowned the shouted orders of the seamen, the lightning reflected from the falling sheets of rain, the young heroes 'coffined in their cabins', praying for death.

> Then note they the ship's sicknesses, the mast
> Shaked with this ague, and the hold and waist
> With a salt dropsy clogged, and all our tacklings
> Snapping, like too-high-stretched treble strings.
> And from our tottered sails, rags drop down so,
> As from one hanged in chains, a year ago.
> Even our ordnance placed for our defence,
> Strive to break loose, and 'scape away from thence.

Donne landed at Plymouth, which was soon full of gloomy soldiers whose funds had run out, and who hung around the ale-houses in their finery trying to drum up credit. On 15 August, after repairs, the fleet set off again, but in much smaller numbers: only a thousand, instead of six thousand, fighting men. They battled through the Bay of Biscay in another storm (the flagship sprang a leak again, and Raleigh's ship lost her mainyard), and paused off Flores, in the Azores, waiting for a sight of the enemy. Now, it was dead calm, and the fleet lay under a bright sun, the heat unmitigated by so much as a breath of wind. Donne, again to his friend Brooke, described *The Calm* in the second of his verse-letters: the pitch between the planks was liquid with the heat, and in the windless air feathers and dust lay in the same place on deck, day after day. Naked men lay prone on the hatches, their tatters of clothes hung on the rigging above them, unmoving in the still air; those of the crew who attempted to cool down by bathing, came out of the sea 'like parboiled wretches' no more refreshed than before.

The expedition was not a very happy one: Donne may (if he was under Raleigh's immediate command) have been present at the capture of Fayal, which was a success; but through a mixture of bad luck and bad planning, there was no major encounter with the Spaniards, and by the end of October the fleet was back in English waters, and Donne had set foot on deck for the last time as a soldier. His travels in future were on less contentious occasions.

At twenty-five, Donne – extremely personable, well educated, somewhat studied in law, with the additional cachet of having taken part in two or three well-publicized military expeditions – now found himself a position which promised him a brilliant future. He became chief secretary to the Lord Keeper of the Great Seal, Sir Thomas Egerton (to whom he was probably introduced by young Thomas

Sir Thomas Egerton, who took Donne 'to be his Chief Secretary; supposing and intending it to be an Introduction to some more weighty Employment in the State; for which, his Lordship did often protest, he thought him very fit'.

The Courts of King's Bench and Chancery met in Westminster Hall.

Egerton, the Keeper's elder son, a fellow student at Lincoln's Inn, who had also been on the expedition to the Azores).

Egerton himself had had an extremely successful career, rising spectacularly from private practice in the law through the positions of Solicitor-General and Attorney-General to Master of the Rolls, and, in 1596, Lord Keeper, in which capacity he presided over the House of Lords and the Court of Star Chamber, and organized the proceedings of the Court of Chancery. What must have been reassuring to Donne was the fact that in his youth Egerton had been a Catholic, once himself summoned before Star Chamber for non-attendance at church, but later reconciled to the establishment.

The Lord Keeper made his home, as was the custom, at York House, a palace in extensive grounds leading down to the north bank of the Thames, where Embankment Gardens now lie. (Inigo Jones's water-gate, still to be seen there, is the only remaining fragment of the original house.) He worked, of course, in the Palace of White-hall – that extraordinary rabbit-warren or rookery which was not only the seat of British government but the social heart of London, perhaps Europe. It was a city within a city, covering twenty-three acres with over two-thousand rooms; and at its centre were the royal apartments – the Presence Chamber, where (at least in James I's time and later)

York house   Durham house   Ivy lane   Bedford howse

Whitehall Bridge   White Hall Stairs

(*Top*) York House, at the centre of the sketch (and *above*), lay next to the Palace of Whitehall. Whitehall Stairs (*left*) gave easy access to the Palace from the Thames.

29

everyone invited to Court was free to walk, and the Privy Chamber, which only the few could enter. The Great Court, the Terrace, the Stone Gallery were busy with courtiers, messengers, even ordinary members of the public, for entry from the river at Whitehall Steps or through the King Street or Holbein Gates was fairly free.

The three chief officers of the Court were the Lord Chamberlain, the Lord Steward and the Master of the Horse. But next to them, and the Earl Marshal, the Lord Keeper took his place with the Lord Treasurer, Lord Privy Seal, Lord President of the Council, and other principal officers of the Crown. Egerton was an important man, and Donne naturally attracted attention as his secretary.

Just before appointing his new assistant, Egerton had remarried after the death of his first wife. The new Lady Egerton was the widow of a Privy Councillor, and had been favourite maid-of-honour of Queen Elizabeth; she commanded a large fortune. The household was a distinguished one, from every point of view; and its younger members – undergraduates and law students – were very much of Donne's cast of mind.

But its most important member, fatal to Donne, was one of the youngest: the fourteen-year-old daughter of Lady Egerton's brother, Sir George More – a good-hearted if splenetic man who from his house at Loseley Park, near Guildford, kept a keen eye on local politics, as well as being a Member of Parliament. He had nine children, of whom only one son survived; of his daughters, Ann was the third, and Lady Egerton accepted her into her family at York House in return for the care her brother had taken in raising and educating her fatherless son Francis (by her previous husband).

Donne, while technically a servant, found no difficulty or embarrassment in making friends with the Lord Keeper's sons, his stepson, or with little Ann More. Izaak Walton records that Egerton did not treat Donne 'so much [as] his Servant, as to forget he was his Friend; and to testify it, did always use him with much courtesy, appointing him a place at his own Table, to which he esteemed his Company and Discourse to be a great Ornament.' He was in a very real sense a part of the family, sharing its grief when Egerton's son, young Sir Thomas, was wounded during his service under Essex in Ireland, and died in Dublin Castle. At his funeral in Chester Cathedral, the young poet bore his dead friend's sword in procession before his coffin.

Life as Egerton's secretary must have been fascinating: not only was there the continual interest of the various law cases in which the Keeper was involved, but there were other matters – matters of State – which were dangerously interesting. Just after the death of young Sir Thomas, Essex had come home from Ireland, against the Queen's express command, and forced his way into her private apartments at

SIR GEORGE MORE

(*Left*) Sir George More, MP for Surrey, who kept a household of fifty servants, including a chaplain, at Loseley. 'By nature very passionate . . . little, and good.'

(*Below*) The north front of Loseley Park, built by Sir Thomas More's kinsman, Sir William More, in 1561–69, partly with stone from Waverley Abbey, near Farnham.

Nonsuch House, Queen Elizabeth's great palace in Surrey, built by Henry VIII, using 'the most outstanding artificers, architects, carvers and sculptors of diverse nations, Italians, Frenchmen, Dutch and men of his own country'. Nothing of it now remains.

Nonsuch House (by legend, finding his white-haired, balding mistress without her wig). Now, he was banished from Court, and placed in Egerton's keeping. He took up residence at York House, for some time ill, depressed, no doubt frightened.

Donne saw him almost every day, and at close quarters found him less the flamboyant hero of tradition. In the meantime, the Court went on its brilliant way as though Essex had never existed: 'no more missed here than the angels which were cast down from heaven, nor (for anything I see) likelier to return', Donne wrote.

In January 1600, while Essex was still at York House, Lady Egerton fell ill and died. The prisoner was sent off to his own home, Essex House (where he was still kept under guard); Francis Wolley (Egerton's stepson) left for Pyrford, in Surrey, which he now in-herited from his mother; Ann More went home to Loseley Park, and her father.

Nine months later, Egerton married for the third time. The new Lady Egerton was the Countess of Derby, whose late husband, the Earl, had been a patron of Spenser, and to whom, in 1633, Milton was to dedicate his *Arcades*. She brought a large train of servants to York House, together with three daughters (who became Donne's friends, and remained so for the rest of his life). And as domestic affairs moved forward, so did national events: Essex gambled on rebellion, was tried, and executed. Donne must have had much to do with the organization of the trial, the preparation of witnesses, and so on. In 1601, he became Member of Parliament for Brackley, in Northamptonshire – a borough in the pocket of the Lord Keeper, who naturally felt that it would be convenient if his secretary was a member of the House of Commons. There is no record that Donne ever spoke in the House; he was there, it seems, purely to serve his master.

It was during this period of his life, or a little earlier, that Donne wrote his first prose pieces – the *Paradoxes* and *Problems*. He spoke slightingly of them: 'they are but swaggerers – quiet enough if you resist them . . . they have only this advantage to scape from being called ill things, that they are nothings.' But this was something of a pose, for he kept commending them to his friends – until his career in the Church made it unwise to draw attention to their corporeal arguments: that, for instance, 'my body licenceth my soul to see the world's beauties through mine eyes; to hear pleasant things through mine ears; and affords it apt Organs for the convenient of all perceivable delight'.

On the whole, these little prose snippets are rather ill tempered, and their occasional flashes of real wit do not make them readily readable; they point but faintly to the marvellous language of Donne's later prose.

It was as Parliament was assembling, in October 1601, that Sir George More brought Ann again to London. And we can fairly assume that Donne's reunion with her was as ecstatic as it was secret, for by this time they must have been violently in love. So little evidence exists as to the progress of their love that conjecture is unsafe; but if they had not been lovers before now, it is highly probable that they soon were. In the sixteenth of his *Elegies*, *On his Mistress*, Donne remembers their first meeting in 1597, the 'desires which thereof did ensue . . . our long starving hopes' and 'that remorse/Which my words' masculine persuasive force/ Begot in thee'. He had perhaps already, then, attempted to seduce her, and she had resisted. In 1601, after a year apart, the force of their mutual passion overwhelmed her objections; or perhaps apart from an irresistible physical urge, they felt a simple strong desire to pledge each other, to engage themselves to marry.

The *sponsalia de praesenti*, a medieval ceremony in which by simply promising marriage, a couple were entitled to live together until the actual ceremony, was still sometimes observed in the England of the late sixteenth century. Though society and the Church disapproved, a pledge of marriage followed by love-making bound lovers to their own satisfaction in a kind of unofficial but effective engagement, and was a sufficient sop to any moral objection to seduction.

In this case, there was, as far as we know, no ceremony before witnesses; but it seems probable that by the time Ann went back to

Sir George More's bedroom at
Loseley Park.

Loseley Park with her father, in December 1601, she was no longer a
virgin. Donne later claimed that by this time they had been secretly
married; but he gives no certain date, and it may be that what really
happened was that in January 1602 Ann got word to him that she
was pregnant, and that he married her soon afterwards, giving the
date as December to protect her reputation (the precise date of birth
of their daughter Constance is unknown; the records which would
have preserved it are lost).

At all events, sometime around the turn of the year, the marriage
took place. Donne's friend Christopher Brooke gave the bride away,
and Brooke's brother Samuel performed the ceremony. There were
two other witnesses.

And now, they had to tell Ann's father. The prospect was a frighten-
ing one. Not only was Sir George extremely short-tempered, but the
couple had really behaved extremely reprehensibly in the eyes of the
society of their time. Ann, now seventeen, was still a minor – not that
she was 'too young' for marriage; many of the sons and daughters of
the nobility and gentry were in their early teens when they went to their
weddings: the Earl of Lichfield was twelve when he married the eleven-
year-old daughter of the Duchess of Cleveland. But Donne, while by

The drawing-room at Loseley. The house has fine ceilings, panelling from Nonsuch House (see p. 32), and a unique chimney-piece carved from local chalk.

no means totally ineligible, was not the kind of man Sir George would automatically have considered a welcome suitor. And apart from that, the very fact that the father had not been consulted (at a time when marriages were still more often than not arranged, or at any rate organized, by the parents of the couple concerned) was outrageous. At last, Donne screwed up his courage to write to his father-in-law.

If ever there was a time when what Izaak Walton calls his 'strange kind of elegant irresistible art' was needed, it was now. At first, it seemed to have no effect whatsoever. He quite naturally (though perhaps unwisely) feared to confront Sir George in person – interestingly, he was suffering from an unspecified illness, no doubt psychosomatic – and instead sent a letter by one of Sir George's friends (no less a person than the Earl of Northumberland) confessing the marriage. There was one reason alone why the couple had not asked Sir George's permission, he said: the fact that they knew they would not get it. Therefore, he naïvely suggested, 'methinks we should be pardoned . . . our fault be but this, that we did not, by fore-revealing of it, consent to our hindrance and torment'.

But he was obviously not very hopeful that this point would tell with Sir George. 'I know this letter shall find you full of passion',

Sr I send yo̅u̅ back by this bearer
the littell b̅ I borrowed of yo̅u̅. If yo̅u̅ wyll
now, to ease my imprisonmt spare me some of
the french negotiacions, wch shall have them
as faythfully kept and as orderly returnd as
these: And when J ame worth yr Comaundinge
J ame whôlly yrs. fro my prison in my
Chamber. 20 febr: 1601
yr honest assured frind
J: Donne

On 20 February 1602, Donne
writes 'from my prison in my
chamber' to Robert Cotton, an
antiquary, asking to borrow a book
to dispel the boredom of
imprisonment.

he frankly admits; adding that 'I know no passion can alter your
reason and wisdom, to which I adventure to commend these parti-
culars: that it is irremediably done; that if you incense my Lord
[Egerton] you destroy her and me; that it is easy to give us happiness,
and that my endeavours and industry, if it please you to prosper them,
may soon make me somewhat worthier of her.'

Sir George's immediate reaction was all Donne feared: fuming with
rage, he sent instantly to the Lord Keeper, demanding Donne's
dismissal and imprisonment. Egerton hesitated over the first point, but
eventually gave his secretary notice; and within a few days both Donne
and Christopher Brooke found themselves in prison, Donne in the
Fleet, and Brooke in the Marshalsea. Fortunately, Egerton was fond
of Donne, and the latter had comparatively little difficulty in securing
his release, at first to his own guarded lodgings, and then to more or
less complete freedom 'to take the air about the town'.

Surprisingly soon, though not too soon for poor Ann, who had to
bear the full brunt of her father's fury, Sir George himself began to
relent. The High Commission, to which he had appealed for an
annulment of the marriage, was fairly obviously going to confirm that
it was valid; and no doubt he was beginning to take Donne's point
that if he was prevented from making his way in the world, Ann would
suffer with him.

But sufficient harm had been done in those first furious days. When
Sir George appealed to Egerton to reinstate Donne as his secretary,
the Lord Keeper was short with him: Walton asserts that he told Sir
George sharply that 'it was inconsistent with his place and credit, to

6° Julij 1602

Receiued the Day and yeur abourwritti of the right ho: Sr Thomas Egerton knight L: keeper of the great Seale of England, my ho: L: and Master by the hands of hys seruant Mr John Panton the sume of one hundred pounds of lawfull money of England: wch sayd hundred pounds was given by the right ho: the Lady Egerton late wyfe to the sayd L: keeper, to her Nece, Anne the Daughter of Sr George Mon, alsso my wyfe, and ys now for her receiued by me

J Donne

Lord Keeper Egerton, to lighten the financial burden of the newly married Donne, ordered the payment of £100 left to Ann by her aunt. Donne's receipt is dated 6 July 1602.

discharge and re-admit servants at the request of passionate petitioners'. Donne, appealing also to his old master, received a dusty answer, and wrote Ann a melancholy letter which he is said to have ended 'John Donne – Ann Donne – Un-done.' (It is fair to say that the pun was probably not Donne's at all, but a current witticism which Walton uncritically reprinted.)

Francis Wolley came forward with an offer of accommodation at Pyrford, and within a few weeks Donne and his wife, reunited, moved there. He was now a man of thirty, without a position, and almost penniless, for the expenses of a suit in the Court of Audience of Canterbury (which had confirmed the legality of the marriage) had cost him most of his remaining inheritance. Though the future prospect was unpromising, the few years the Donnes spent in the pleasant, old half-timbered house near Loseley Park will not have been entirely unhappy. They were deeply in love – and soon started a family: as we have seen, their first child, Constance, was born within a year, and a son, John, in the spring of 1604.

It has been suggested that Donne's marriage was the most unwise action of his life – one he soon bitterly regretted, and continued to regret. This is an over-simplification of a complex psychological reaction. Though the marriage began with his imprisonment, and continued in poverty (which it had provoked), it is still true that at Ann's death fifteen years later Donne was to be (in Walton's words) 'crucified to the world' in a total access of grief, which turned his mind perhaps for the first time wholly to spiritual matters – as he puts it in the magnificent sonnet in her memory:

Part of the map of Surrey completed in 1598 by the topographer John Norden. Pyrford, within its enclosure, is at the bottom left of the map, numbered *12*.

Since she whom I lov'd hath paid her last debt
To nature, and to hers, and my good is dead,
And her soul early into heaven ravished,
Wholly in heavenly things my mind is set.

Several of the best of Donne's love poems, too, testify to the love which remained firmly focused on Ann throughout their life together – and indeed their lives when they were apart. Suggestions have been made that Donne was unfaithful to his wife, certainly in mind, and perhaps in body. They are unsupported by real evidence, and denied by the tone of the love poems which, though they *may* have been inspired by other women, are much more likely to have been a celebration of his love for Ann. While it would be stupid to suppose that a man with as strong an erotic drive as Donne could suddenly become immune to the attractions of any body but his wife's, it would be equally silly to assume that he naturally took advantage of his absence from her to make love to any woman who found him sufficiently attractive.

Part of Ann's own attraction for him may well have been her innocence: more than once, he compares her to an angel ('I thought thee an Angel at first sight'), and at thirty, strong-willed and extremely intelligent, he would have been able to mould the naturally intelligent but malleable mind of a girl of seventeen until she became almost like one of his poems, peculiarly his own – the feat Milton must have hoped to perform with Mary Powell forty years later.

Ann also had twelve children in fifteen years, not counting miscarriages; if to nothing else, this fact testifies that the physical bond between them was a lasting one. (It does not testify, as again has been suggested, that Donne was a sadist, forcing his attentions on his wife when he knew that she was physically weak; continual pregnancy was a commonplace of life at a time when love-making all too often resulted in procreation; and there is no reason to believe that Ann ever appealed to her husband to show restraint, or that his passion for her was not wholly reciprocated.)

The marriage of John and Ann Donne is on the evidence we have one of the most ideal and complete in the history of the institution; never was a couple more truly one flesh – that was an ideal Donne had always had, in his attitude to love, and it is revealed in the poems written both before and after his marriage. In *The Canonization*, he sees Ann and himself as one being, a Phoenix; in his most sensual poems – *To his mistress going to bed*, for example – he celebrates the almost magical marriage of the spirit and the flesh which illuminates the moment of orgasm.

> *Licence my roving hands, and let them go,*
> *Before, behind, between, above, below.*
> *O my America! my new found land,*
> *My kingdom, safeliest when with one man manned,*
> *My mine of precious stones, my empery,*
> *How blessed am I in this discovering thee!*
> *To enter in these bonds, is to be free;*
> *Then where my hand is set, my seal shall be.*

This is strongly in contrast with the post-coital melancholy of such poems as *Farewell to love*, in which the magic did not take hold.

Of course, there were times of irritation in his marriage, when the noise and distraction of a growing family of children prevented him from working, and when perhaps Ann herself (incapable, whatever her intelligence, charm and appeal, of joining him in intellectual speculation) jarred. But there can be little doubt that his marriage on the whole was the great illumination and joy of his life; after it ended, much changed. The virile sexual expression which filled so much of his being, and which had been a part of his spiritual life too ('Love's mysteries in souls do grow,/But yet the body is his book') was idealized and turned to the love of Christ – a metamorphosis not impossible to credit, or even to understand, yet surely enormously difficult to accomplish while keeping a crystal-clear sanity and a perfect emotional balance.

Donne's marriage to Ann acted as a direct channel for his spiritual growth; as a man, just as a poet, he reached the spiritual heights of his last years by human, material means – the point at which his sensual instincts became spiritual, immaterial ones, may seem to arrive suddenly (with Ann's death); but it was a journey which took fifteen years, and which could scarcely have been made without her.

Ann's common-sense attitude to life must have counted for much during the difficult early years of their marriage, when Donne, whatever his hopes, had no immediate prospect of preferment, and must have been irritated and saddened by the life lost to him – removal from London and the centre of affairs; the loss of friends and their daily company and conversation, which letters could not replace.

(*Opposite*) Paris in the sixteenth century. Francis I's decision to live in the city had resulted in much rebuilding and replanning; it was, too, a centre of intellectual life, of fashion and elegance.

The head of the funeral procession of Elizabeth I. 'She knew the world would talk of her after her death, and therefore she did such things all her life were worthy to be talked of.'

There was perhaps a shred of hope when, after the Donnes had been at Pyrford for less than a year, Queen Elizabeth died, and James I made a progress which brought him to stay for one night with Francis Wolley. James certainly heard the story of Donne's unwise marriage, and remembered it; it was clear that there was no hope of a position at Court, even during the inevitable juggling for position which took place during the setting up of the new régime.

After two years of contemplative life at Pyrford, Donne suddenly – in February 1605 – applied for and obtained a licence to travel abroad for three years, with a companion, two servants, four horses, and a specified amount of money. The companion was a slightly younger man, Sir Walter Chute, who Donne presumably got to know on the Azores expedition, of which he had been a member. They travelled together in Europe for about a year – certainly to Paris, possibly to Venice and Rome; but we know nothing for certain about the tour or its object (if it had any). Donne was back in England by the beginning of April 1606, for a son, Francis, was born nine months later and baptized on 8 January 1607. The birth had taken place at Peckham, where Ann spent the months of her husband's absence with his sister Lady Grymes.

Now, a real reconciliation took place between the couple and Sir George More, who relented at last to the extent of giving Donne a regular allowance of £20 a quarter, as interest on a postponed dowry of £800. On the strength of this small but regular income, Donne felt able to rent a modest house at Mitcham, within easy reach of London, and before the end of the year had moved into it with his wife and three sons. There, he settled down to hours of regular work as a writer – of a number of poems, but also of three substantial prose

The Hors: trapped to th velvett led by two Querries

The Sergeant of the vestrie

of the Chappell.

Gentlemen of the
Chappell.

Clarks

Deputie Clarke of the
Markett
Clarks extraordinary
Cofferer
Dyett.

To the Noblest knight
Sr Edward Herbert.

Sr

I make account that thys Booke hath mough per=
form'd wch yt undertooke, both by Argument and
Example. Itt shall therfore the Lesse neede to bee
ytt selfe another Example of ye Doctrine. Itt shall
not therfore kyll yttselfe, that ys, not bury it selfe,
for if ytt should do so, those reasons by wch that
Act should bee defended or excus'd, were also lost
wt ytt. Since ytt ys content to liue, ytt camot
chuse a wholsomer ayre then yor Library, where
Autors of all complexions are preserud. If any
of them grudge thys Booke a roome, and sus=
pect ytt of new or dangerous doctrine, yow who
know us all, can best Moderate. To those reasons,
wch I know yor Loue to mee wyll make in my fauer,
and dischardge, yow may add thys, That though
thys Doctrine hath not beene tought nor defen=
ded by writers, yet they, most of any sorte of Men
in the world, haue practisd ytt. — — —

yor very true and earnest
frinde and seruant
and Louer

J Donne

Donne's house at Mitcham, demolished in the 1840s, was approached down an avenue of yew trees.

works, *Biathanatos* (in which he grappled with the notion of suicide, 'that self-homicide is not so naturally sin, that it may never be otherwise'), *Ignatius his Conclave* (a fantasy devoted mainly to denigrating the Jesuits), and *Pseudo-Martyr*, his best-known work in prose.

He worked in a small damp study just above the cellar of the Mitcham house (the hours he spent there did not help his health, which was never robust), and as he wrote contemplated what still – despite the slight amelioration of his circumstances – seemed a bleak future: so bleak that it is not surprising that his thoughts turned to suicide. In two of his *Paradoxes*, he had argued that suicide was natural, that 'all things kill themselves' – the finest plants dying earliest, the most thoroughbred of racehorses killing themselves by their own exertions. Now, in *Biathanatos*, he argued much more seriously that man should be allowed to put an end to his miseries. In the preface, he wrote that indeed he had often thought of doing so: 'whensoever any affliction assails me, methinks I have the keys of my prison in my own hand, and no remedy presents itself so soon to my heart, as my own sword'.

He had not entirely given up the idea of securing some public appointment: he applied, through a friend, for a position in the Queen's household – but it came to nothing. Then his name was put before the King as a possible candidate for the vacant position of one of the King's secretaries in Ireland. But James still felt that the circumstances of his marriage made him unsuitable.

Donne dedicated his *Biathanatos* to Sir Edward Herbert. In the dedicatory letter (*opposite*) he already had some misgivings about the book's contents, but 'Since ytt ys content to liue, ytt cannot chuse a wholsomer ayre then yor Library; where Autors of all complexions are preserved.'

Two portraits of Lucy Harrington, Countess of Bedford – one *c.* 1605, the other (*opposite*) later. *If good and lovely were not one, of both | You were the transcript, and original, | The elements, the parent, and the growth, | And every piece of you, is both their all : | So entire are all your deeds, and you, that you | Must do the same thing still; you cannot two.*

Next, he tried what patronage could do. His close friend Sir Henry Goodyer, a Gentleman of the King's Privy Chamber, introduced him to Lucy, Countess of Bedford, one of the Ladies of the Bedchamber to the Queen, and because of her position and aided by her wit and charm, one of the most influential women in England.

Lucy was, in 1607 (when she bought Twickenham Park and set up house there), a beautiful woman of twenty-six whose intelligence matched Donne's own; and soon he began addressing verses to her, in one of the earliest of them declaring that her virtues were such that he was bound to attempt to preserve them in poetry for 'future times'. A common enough conceit – but Donne's admiration for his Countess was real enough: 'Madam, You have refined me,' he declares, and while he also asserts that through her influence he has turned from writing erotic love poems to composing verses of spiritual affirmation, it is possible to discern the old note of physical attraction not far below the surface. He was still a handsome young man, only in his mid-thirties, and no mean figure to have in attendance on one. But such poems as *Twicknam Garden*, a weak and self-conscious piece, show by their manner (substantially different from the earlier poems) that the 'affair', if it can be called so, was platonic. In August 1608 she became godmother to his newborn daughter, who was christened, after her,

45

Elizabeth Stanley, Countess of
Huntingdon: *By virtue's beams by
fame derived from you, | May apt souls,
and the worst may, virtue know.*

John Norden's map (1593) shows
the Strand, connecting the Palace of
Westminster to the City of London.

Lucy. He was almost her poet laureate, turning out rather tedious
elegies on two of her friends who died, and exchanging verse-letters
with her.

But she did not seem willing to advance him in any practical way,
or perhaps was incapable; and it was possibly for that reason that he
accepted a hint from Goodyer that he should write a complimentary
set of verses to the Countess of Huntingdon, who had apparently
shown some interest in him. Donne, though he did write to Lady
Huntingdon, felt it unwise to cultivate two countesses at once. On
the other hand, he did not hesitate to befriend other ladies – Magdalen
Herbert, for instance, whose eldest son Edward was a ward of Sir
George More. Mrs Herbert had met Donne in London, when he was
at York House, and he had written an elegy – *The Autumnal* – to her.
It is a beautiful, but perhaps mildly unflattering poem, alluding quite
frankly to Mrs Herbert's 'autumnal face', her wrinkles, her lack of
voluptuousness. (She was thirty-two when the poem was written!)
Now, in 1607, he began seeing her regularly (he had lodgings in the
Strand, where he stayed on frequent visits to London), wrote her
several poems, and obviously felt a strong attachment, though not one,
Walton insists, 'that polluted their Souls'. Their friendship was only
to end with her death.

Through Mrs Herbert, Donne met Bridget White, a young girl
who appealed to him, again, because of her liveliness and wit ('your
going away hath made London a dead carcass', he wrote to her, '. . .
and I think the only reason why the plague is somewhat slackened
is because the place is dead already, and no body left worth the killing.')

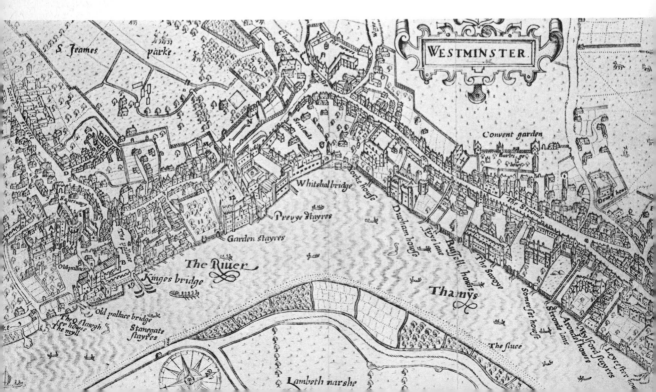

After Bridget White married, Donne continued to keep in touch with her.

Apart from a friendship with Mrs Herbert's eldest son, later Lord Herbert of Cherbury (the diplomat, historian, philosopher and poet), Donne gained nothing from his attachment to these ladies, except the pleasure of their company. They (and we) gained the poems he wrote them, of course – and these demonstrate the changing temper of his emotions. The first year at Pyrford, it seems, was largely given to theological considerations; and these were to be more and more in the forefront of his mind – not only because his mind was predisposed to them, but because events too forced him to give them precedence.

In June 1607 the King appointed Thomas Morton as Dean of Gloucester. Donne had probably met Morton at Cambridge, and must at any rate have heard of his progress in the Church – Chaplain to the Earl of Rutland, author of a book arguing (patiently and without spleen) the case of the Church of England against the Catholics, and of another attacking the more extreme polemics of the Jesuits, at the time of the Gunpowder Plot. Soon after his appointment to Gloucester, Morton sent for Donne, and according to Walton offered him an immediate benefice if he would take Holy Orders.

Sir Edward, Lord Herbert of Cherbury. As a poet, he was much indebted to Donne's influence. *Actions are authors, and of those in you | Your friends find every day a mart of new.*

It seems a very sudden offer: but Walton suggests (and he based his account on a conversation with Morton) that the Dean had often previously attempted to persuade Donne to give up his hopes of preferment at Court, and go into the Church. Donne considered the offer for three days, and then decided against it, explaining to the Dean that far from thinking himself 'too good for that calling, for which Kings, if they think so, are not good enough', he felt that 'some irregularities of my life have been so visible to some men, that though I have, I thank God, made my peace with Him by penitential resolutions against them, and by the assistance of His Grace banished them my affections; yet this, which God knows to be so, is not so visible to man, as to free me from their censures, and it may be that sacred calling from a dishonour.'

Though he may still have been hoping for a successful secular career, it is no doubt also true that Donne honestly felt that some wilder incidents of his youth disqualified him from commanding respect as a priest (perhaps too his efforts to 'banish them his affections' were not entirely as successful as he claimed). The circulation in manuscript of some of the more openly erotic poems would certainly weigh against him, though the publication of *Pseudo-Martyr* would bring him respect, not only in the eyes of laymen in general, but of the Church and the King.

It may also be fair to point out that unless one could be sure of preferment, the Church was no career for a man with any eye to the comforts of life. Archbishop John Whitgift had recently pointed out

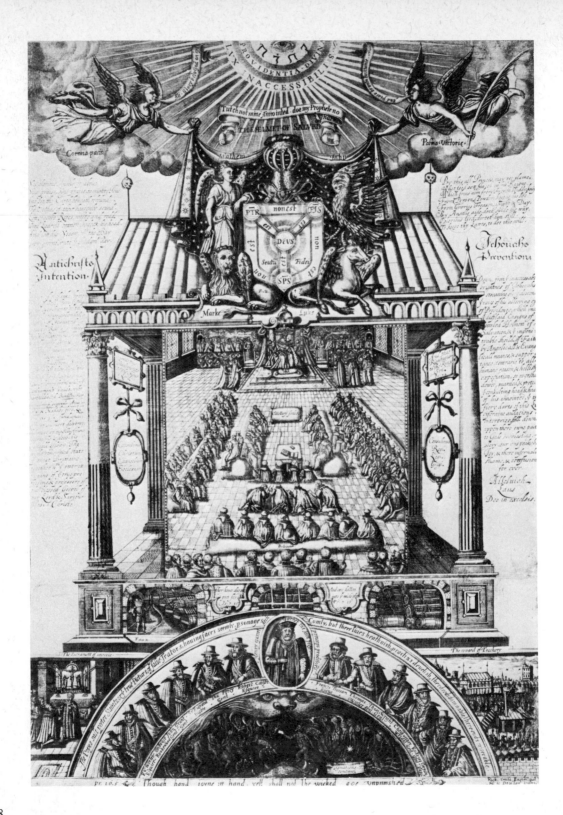

that half of the country's clergy had incomes of under £10 a year. Often much under. On the other hand, many of them had little or no training for their work, and less than half of them had actually been licensed to preach. Donne, of course, would have started with considerable advantages. But it is at least possible that one of the reasons for his lack of enthusiasm may have been a doubt that he could make what in his view would be an adequate living in the Church.

His natural interest in the continuing conflict between Catholics and Protestants had been sharpened by the new penalties devised by Parliament to force Catholics to swear the Oath of Allegiance to James, which not only acknowledged him as Sovereign, but denied the Pope the power to depose him, or to absolve any of his subjects from taking the Oath. One of its clauses (provoked, as the new legislation was, by the Gunpowder Plot, which had been uncovered while Donne was out of the country) insisted that the subscriber did 'from his heart abhor, detest and abjure as impious and heretical, this damnable doctrine and position, that princes which be excommunicated or deprived by the Pope may be deposed or murdered by their subjects'.

This was deeply offensive to Catholics, but understandable – for a survey undertaken just after James came to the throne revealed that there were almost 9000 Catholics in England, and that the number was increasing. Catholics were already forbidden to travel further than five miles from their homes without permission, and were fined for attending Mass; now they were to be forced to attend the services of the Protestant Church, and to take its sacrament. A Catholic declining to take the new Oath would be prevented from approaching within ten miles of London (unless by way of trade), and forced to

The Gunpowder Plot. Michael Droeshout, the engraver of the famous first portrait of Shakespeare, made *The Powder Treason* (*opposite*) to illustrate the enormity of the crimes of the plotters who (*above*) were executed with the utmost ferocity, not at Tyburn but on the piazza at the west end of St Paul's Cathedral, on 30 January 1606.

49

A Catholic Council in England. 'Your Majesty's ill-affected subjects at home, the popish recusants, have taken too much encouragement, and are dangerously increased in their number and in their insolencies.'

apply directly to the Privy Council for permission to travel outside the five-mile boundary. The Catholic became a second-class citizen, and it must be said that it was no help when Pope Paul V disowned any member of the faith who took the new Oath, despite the fact that some of his priests were advising their congregations to do so.

Soon there was open opposition to the Oath. Izaak Walton claims that the King himself commanded Donne to write a defence of it. More likely, *Pseudo-Martyr* was first written and then presented to the King after its publication in 1610. It sets out a cogent argument in favour of Catholics taking the Oath, and claims that those who refused to do so, and suffered for it, were not entitled to be regarded as martyrs – were, in fact, the pseudo-martyrs of the book's title.

It is a well-argued and convincing work, and by no means un-sympathetic to the Catholics, with whom Donne obviously had some fellow feeling. But, familiar with Catholic doctrine since his child-hood, he now set out to make it quite clear that 'the Roman religion doth by many erroneous doctrines misencourage and excite men to this vicious affectation of danger'; that the Jesuits in particular were responsible for the deaths of martyrs; and that while 'it becomes not me to say that the Roman religion begets treason . . . I may say that within one generation it degenerates into it.'

While some readers disliked *Pseudo-Martyr* for not going far enough, and others for its alleged anti-Catholicism, it was on the whole well received – the author was granted an honorary MA by Oxford University, and the King was much impressed.

Good Friday, 1613: Riding Westward has generally been attributed to the date given in its title. The dramatic discovery in 1974 of a hitherto unknown manuscript of this poem (in a collection of papers from Kimbolton Castle, now in the Huntingdon Records Office) suggests otherwise. Donne's poems, during his lifetime, circulated in manuscript; the Huntingdon copy of *Good Friday* is possibly in the hand of Sir Nathanial Rich, an acquaintance of the poet, and it is headed *Meditation upon a Good friday, riding from London towards Exeter, Westward.*

Discussion about the provenance of the manuscript will doubtless go on for some time; but it has been suggested that the heading refers to a journey Donne may have made to see Matthew Sutcliffe, then Dean of Exeter, about the foundation of a college at Chelsea, in 1610 – when Good Friday fell on 6 April, eleven days before Donne went to Oxford to receive his honorary MA.

Read in the light of this possible new dating, the poem certainly seems to comment on Donne's perplexities and worries about whether or not to enter the Church: the King's reaction to *Pseudo-Martyr* had not been an offer of a secular post, but further encouragement to become an ecclesiastic. Donne was still worried about his past misbehaviour:

> *O Saviour, as thou hang'st upon the tree;*
> *I turn my back on thee, but to receive*
> *Corrections, till thy mercies bid thee leave.*
> *O think me worth thine anger, punish me,*
> *Burn off my rusts, and my deformity,*
> *Restore thine image, so much, by thy grace,*
> *That thou mayst know me, and I'll turn my face.*

The last five words prove to have new significance; and indeed, Donne was turning his thoughts more and more to divine matters – it seems to have been at this time that he composed his *Essays in Divinity* – meditations, prayers, essays of various lengths on thoughts arising from the first verse of each of the first two books of the Bible. In the *Essays*, we find some of the most beautiful of his early prose.

Meanwhile, he was dividing his time between Mitcham and London. In the country, he tried hard to conceal from Ann both impatience at his inability to find a position in public life, and his difficulty in setting to work at home in the presence of seven children (for Lucy, Bridget and Mary had followed, at approximately annual intervals, Constance, John, George and Francis). From his fireside, he wrote to Goodyer

in the noise of three gamesome children, and by the side of her whom, because I have transplanted into a wretched fortune, I must labour to disguise that from her by all such honest devices, as giving her my company and discourse; therefore I steal from her all the time which I give this letter, and it is therefore that I take so short a list, and gallop so fast over it. I have not been out of my house since I received your packet. As I have so much quenched my senses, and disused my body from pleasure, and so tried how I can endure to be mine own grave, so I try now how I can suffer a prison.

His visits to London must have been a great relief to him, however loving he was to Ann (already suffering from constant childbearing). The Mitcham house was to him a prison, 'a dungeon'; and the most devoted husband might be excused for constantly having in mind the fact that less than two hours away was the Mitre Tavern, where the entertaining wit and traveller Thomas Coryate, the architect Inigo

Thomas Coryate published one of the earliest, and most entertaining, of all travel books. His friend Donne paid him a back-handed compliment: *Thy giant wit o'erthrows me, I am gone: And rather than read all, I would read none.*

Ben Jonson, who admired *Donne, the delight of Phoebus, and each Muse . . . Whose every work, of thy most early wit | Came forth example, and remains so, yet.*

Jones, the poets Ben Jonson and Michael Drayton, George Chapman (the translator of Homer), and many of Donne's old friends from the Inns of Court regularly met at an informal club. There he could talk, extemporize verses, relax in an atmosphere nearer that of the university or the Court (or those later days at York House) than he could find anywhere else.

Donne always preferred the hustle and bustle of the city to the quiet of the country: he found what quiet he needed in his study, and within the bone walls of his skull. When he went out of doors, he liked to find himself in busy streets, where 'carts and coaches make such a thundering as if the world ran upon wheels', as Thomas Dekker described them: where

at every corner men, women and children meet in such shoals, that posts are set up on purpose to strengthen the houses, lest with jostling one another they should shoulder them down. Besides hammers are beating in one place, tubs hooping in another, pots clinking in a third, water tankards running at tilt

'London is a very populous city, so that one can scarcely pass along the streets, on account of the throng. The inhabitants are magnificently apparelled, and are extremely proud and overbearing. . . . The women have much more liberty than perhaps in any other place; they also know well how to make use of it.'

in a fourth. Here are porters sweating under burdens, there merchants' men bearings bags of money. Chapmen (as if they were at leap frog) skip out of one shop into another. Tradesmen (as if they were dancing galliards) are lusty at legs and never stand still. All are as busy as country attorneys at an assizes.

The scene was inspiriting and enlivening. Mitcham was not.

But sobriety predominated in Donne's inner life, as can be seen in the *Holy Sonnets*, *A Litany* and *La Corona*, all written in this period. The sonnets reveal, indeed, additional reasons which weighed with him against entering the Church. Despair (regarded as a sin) had beaten him down, and fear of death was closing in on him – 'Despair behind, and death before doth cast/Such terror' – so that at times he became almost manic-depressive because of authority's refusal to consider him fit to serve King or country, and his own refusal to consider himself fit to serve God. Every avenue seemed blocked which might have led him from the prison of his 'low devout melancholy'.

Even the most magnificent of his sonnets, in part triumphant shouts of affirmation and joy, have a dying fall. One of the most famous begins:

> At the round earth's imagined corners, blow
> Your trumpets, angels, and arise, arise
> From death, you numberless infinities
> Of souls, and to your scattered bodies go,
> All whom the flood did, and fire shall o'erthrow,
> All whom war, dearth, age, agues, tyrannies,
> Despair, law, chance, hath slain, and you whose eyes
> Shall behold God, and never taste death's woe.

But then comes the realization of the writer's own need for grace, redemption from sin:

> But let them sleep, Lord, and me mourn a space,
> For, if above all these, my sins abound,
> 'Tis late to ask abundance of thy grace,
> When we are there; here on this lowly ground,
> Teach me how to repent; for that's as good
> As if thou hadst sealed my pardon, with thy blood.

Fortuitously, it was at this time – early in 1611, when Donne's melancholy was beginning to prove most trying – that he was taken up by a man whose friendship was to be a turning-point in his life: Sir Robert Drury (knighted on the battlefield when he was only fifteen), whose taste for plain speaking and lack of real intelligence had barred him from high office, but who was an honourable and respected landowner. Donne may have known Drury for some years, but it was the beautiful memorial elegy he wrote on the death of Elizabeth Drury that brought them together.

Elizabeth, a beautiful girl of fourteen, was Drury's only surviving child. She died on the eve of the Feast of St Lucy, and this fact (together with the waste of her death on the eve of her marriage) struck to Donne's heart. *A Funeral Elegy* is not only fine in itself, but led Donne on to the *Anniversaries*, which are among his best poems.

Drury, perhaps to muffle the shock of his daughter's death, was planning a European tour, and invited Donne to accompany him, perhaps chiefly as interpreter. Ann protested: the journey might last for years, she was ill and yet again pregnant. But Donne was persuasive, and at last she consented. So sending her and the children to her younger sister on the Isle of Wight, he set out with Drury for Amiens, where it was proposed to spend the winter.

Donne began the journey in an unsettled frame of mind: not only was he still without prospects, and in debt to Goodyer and others, but Ann's illness and sorrow at their parting deeply disturbed him – he wrote two poems to her, in an attempt to console her: *A Valediction: forbidding mourning*, and the song 'Sweetest love, I do not go,/For weariness of thee . . .'

> *Let not they divining heart*
> *Forethink me any ill,*
> *Destiny may take thy part,*
> *And may thy fears fulfil;*
> *But think that we*
> *Are but turned aside to sleep;*
> *They who one another keep*
> *Alive, ne'er parted be.*

By December, the coach and twelve horses had carried Sir Robert, his wife and Donne to the house in Amiens which had been lent them; the party included servants and outriders, and was followed by a pack of hounds and a few hawks (Sir Robert was hoping to see some sport). Donne spent the time studying, writing letters home, and worrying – about his future, about Ann. There was not enough variety in his life at Amiens to occupy him: this was not what he had come abroad for (though once more, his reasons for travelling at all seem uncertain). Tension eventually upset his constitution, so that when the party went to Paris in March, he suffered 'such storms of a stomach colic as kept me in a continual vomiting, so that I know not what I should have been able to do to dispatch this wind. . . .'

In April, he was severely disturbed by lack of news of his family: 'I have received no syllable,' he told Goodyer, 'neither from herself nor by any others, how my wife hath passed her danger – nor do I know whether I be increased by a child, or diminished by the loss of a wife.' Then came the famous vision which he saw in his chamber, of his wife 'with her hair hanging about her shoulders, and a dead child in her arms'. He was certain, he told Drury, that it was not a dream; and a messenger from London soon informed him that (as Walton reports) Ann had given birth to a dead child 'the same day, and about the very hour that Mr Donne assumed he saw her pass by in his Chamber'. Donne seems to have been in a low state of health, and in such a highly wrought state of nervous tension that if ever he was to see visions, it was an apt time. Walton heard the story from apparently impeccable sources, and it was a common anecdote for some years subsequently, though later biographers (R. C. Bald, in particular) have claimed that a close examination of the dates of the vision and of Ann's miscarriage, together with the time a messenger would spend on a journey from England to France, suggest that the vision did not occur at the same time as the abortion. However, the episode is certainly an indication of Donne's acute imaginative sensitivity.

Paris, even if one was unwell, was a great deal livelier than Amiens. Donne interested himself, for instance, in the current dispute there between the theologians of the Sorbonne and some Jesuit scholars who had been arguing the Pope's authority over secular kings: indeed, he was ready to join in, but perhaps fortunately circum-stances precluded it. Then there were secular pleasures: crowds had converged on the capital for the joint betrothals of Louis XIII and Anne of Austria, and Louis's sister and the heir to the Spanish throne. There were processions and brave shows to see.

Louis XIII succeeded to the throne at the age of nine, a year before Donne's second visit to Paris. Anne of Austria was to marry him in 1615; the marriage was ruined by the machinations of Cardinal Richelieu.

The 'Carrousel' held in Paris on
5, 6 and 7 April 1612, in celebration
of the betrothals of Louis XIII and
his sister. Over 200,000 people
crowded into stands and marquees.
'The main bravery was the number
of horses, which were above 800
caparisoned.'

58

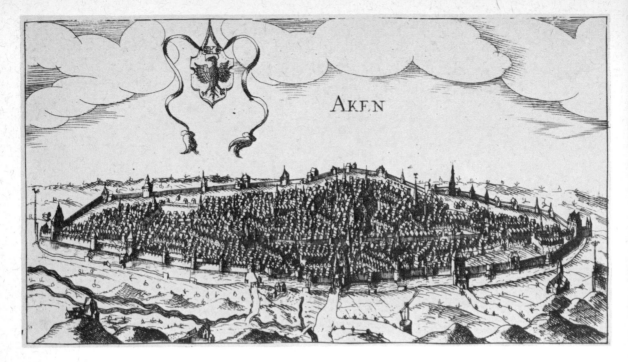

AKEN

Aix, or Aachen, its cathedral founded in 796 by Charlemagne, whose body, seated on a marble throne and dressed in magnificent robes, was removed from his tomb to a shrine in 1000.

At the end of April, the English party set off for Heidelberg and Frankfurt, staying *en route* at Aix. In a sermon, Donne later recalled his stay there:

I found myself in a house which was divided into many families, and indeed so large as it might have been a little parish, or at least a great limb of a great one; but it was of no parish: for when I asked who lay over my head, they told me a family of Anabaptists; and who over theirs? – another family of Anabaptists; and another family of Anabaptists over theirs; and the whole house was a nest of these boxes – several artificers; all Anabaptists; I asked in what room they met for the exercise of their religion; I was told they never met: for, though they were all Anabaptists, yet for some collateral differences they detested one another, and, though many of them were near in blood and alliance to one another, yet the son would excommunicate the father, in the room above him, and the nephew the uncle.

At Spa, which they reached by mid July, there was a large colony of expatriate Englishmen and women, as well as some visiting the town to take the waters (which had been famous since the fourteenth century). So there was some social life. But by now, Donne was all impatience to be home. There had been some interesting incidents during the journey, he had seen some unusual sights (had attended a Jewish synagogue, for instance), but he was looking forward to the trip by barge down the River Maas, then home through Holland. This was denied him: the river was too low. And so they went by road to Brussels, then homeward, and 'sneaked into London' by the beginning of September.

The excursion had not been as pleasant or as useful as Donne may have expected. True, we do not know precisely what his expectations were, but since there was no practical benefit to him of any kind, we may assume that he was disappointed. There was one happy result of his friendship with Drury, however: Sir Robert rented him, very reasonably, a neat little brick house attached to his own mansion in Drury Lane, with a private entrance to a paved court within the larger courtyard of Drury House itself. Donne moved his family into this new home towards the end of 1612 or at the beginning of 1613. The two elder boys could now go to school in London (John, to Westminster), and the other five children had a great deal more room than at the little cottage at Mitcham. Nicholas joined them in August 1613 and was baptized at St Clement Danes, though he apparently died in infancy.

No doubt Donne was delighted with his new home. But there were some disadvantages: several Catholics were believed to live in the Drury Lane area, which was soon to be known as 'Little Rome'; and Donne himself may not have felt above suspicion, for his step⁄

London in about 1636, as seen by Wenceslaus Hollar. Drury Lane curves down from left to right of the prospect. Within Drury House stood 'one bricke howse in the tenure of Mr Doctor Dunn with a little passage and a smale Court to the same belonginge.'

Sir Robert Ker, Viscount Rochester,
Earl of Somerset (*top*), and James,
Lord Hay, Viscount Doncaster.

father Richard Rainsford (his mother's third husband, whom she had married in about 1590) was now in Newgate Prison, convicted during Donne's absence abroad for that very refusal to subscribe to the Oath of Allegiance which Donne had condemned in *Pseudo-Martyr*. It was very likely, however, that his book had cleared Donne of any real suspicion of papist sympathies; and now, he decided to make one more great effort to capture a respectable post about the Court.

While he was at Frankfurt, he had heard the news of the death of the Earl of Salisbury, the secretary and confidant of the King. No new secretary had been appointed, and James was coming more and more to rely on the advice and assistance of Robert Ker, Viscount Rochester. One of Rochester's friends had also been a friend of Donne's: James, Lord Hay, a good-looking dandy who was very popular about the Court, and had once tried to help Donne by urging his appointment as secretary in Ireland. Now, he agreed to present to Rochester a letter of appeal from the poet.

The letter was unspecific, simply pleading for Rochester's 'favourable assistance'. But it reached the Court at precisely the right moment: Rochester had just had his former friend Sir Thomas Overbury committed to the Tower of London for obstructing his plan to marry Frances Howard, Countess of Essex. Overbury had to all intents and purposes been Rochester's secretary, and the latter was now looking for someone to take his place. Donne was introduced, and Rochester found him intelligent, able, and no doubt willing. He certainly did not become, officially, Rochester's secretary; indeed, we do not know what work he performed in response to the financial aid Rochester gave him; but we do know that he defended the peculiarly unpleasant divorce of the Earl of Essex and his wife, and that when Rochester – by then created Earl of Somerset – married the lady in December 1613, the poet wrote a sycophantic and not very good *Eclogue and Epithalamion* marking the occasion. Well, he had his way to make, and a large family to support.

There is no satisfactory defence to be made against the accusation that Donne was now more intent than ever on ingratiating himself with anyone who might be of use to him. He had been neglecting his old patron and friend Lady Bedford for some time, though he must have known that she had been gravely ill, and that her husband, thrown from his horse, had been paralysed. Now, hearing that her brother, 'the most complete young gentleman of his age that this kingdom could afford for religion, learning and courteous behaviour', had died of smallpox at only twenty-one, Donne felt that the time was ripe for a new approach, and sent her a long poem in which he rehearsed the young man's interests and preoccupations, together with a letter tactlessly alluding to his fortune, and soliciting a gift.

The Earl and Countess of Somerset.
This is joy's bonfire, then, where love's strong arts | Make of so noble individual parts | One fire of four inflaming eyes, and of two loving hearts.

Wenceslaus Hollar's view of the Tower of London.

In 1613 and 1614, Donne paid some court to Lady Huntingdon, and sent some verses to the Countess of Salisbury: 'Fair, great and good . . . your beauty shines . . . you come to repair God's book of creatures, teaching what is fair. . . .' None of these ladies was of practical help.

If this is the period of Donne's life during which his behaviour can be most easily criticized, there are certain excuses to be made. He was, for instance, very unwell. He was having trouble with his eyes, and describes himself in a letter as 'at least half-blind'; then, as he began to improve, Ann had a miscarriage, and all the children fell mysteriously ill. Donne nursed them virtually single-handed, then, when they recovered, himself fell ill again, and Ann – who had been miming better health so as not to distress him further – suffered a relapse. Donne wrote to Goodyer:

My wife hath now confessed herself to be extremely sick; she hath held out thus long to assist me, but is now overturned, and here we be in two beds, or graves; so that God hath marked out a great many of us, but taken none yet. I have passed ten days without taking anything; so that I think no man can live more thriftily. I have purged and vexed my body much since I writ to you, and this day I have missed my fit, and this is the first time that I could discern any intermission.

Before he was much better, Mary, his three-year-old daughter, died.

The pressures of illness, lack of prospects and penury – he had been forced to give up keeping a horse, and to borrow one when he had to travel – compelled him to indulge in sycophancy and begging (not so shameful, in the seventeenth century, as it seems to us). The fact that his friends still liked and admired him, showing no signs of rejecting his company, seems to say that he retained a sense of humour, and was at least not reduced to begging from them.

It was at this time that he wrote the last of his great erotic poems, the St Valentine's Day *Epithalamion*. The *Epithalamion*, written for the marriage of the eldest daughter of James I and Frederick, the Elector Palatine, is certainly the best of the many poems written by various hands for the occasion:

> *Here lies a she sun, and a he moon here,*
> > *She gives the best light to his sphere,*
> > *Or each is both, and all, and so*
> *They unto one another nothing owe,*
> > *And yet they do, but are*
> *So just and rich in that coin, which they pay,*
> *That neither would, nor needs forbear, nor stay;*
> *Neither desires to be spared, nor to spare,*
> > *They quickly pay their debt, and then*
> *Take no acquittances, but pay again;*

They pay, they give, they lend, and so let fall
No such occasion to be liberal.
More truth, more courage in these two do shine,
Than all thy turtles have, and sparrows, Valentine.

And by this act of these two phoenixes
  Nature again restored is,
  For since these two are two no more,
There's but one phoenix still, as was before. . . .

The uncertainties of the past few years had been unsettling: but at least there seemed to be some hope of an improvement in Donne's material position in 1614, when he was returned Member of Parliament for Taunton (a borough in the pocket of Sir Edward Phelips, Master of the Rolls, whose son he had known in the circle at the Mitre). But the Parliament he joined was the 'Addled Parliament', which sat for only two months, and passed no Bills at all, spending its time in sterile argument and nit-picking. There is no record of Donne having uttered a single word during the Parliament's short

James I in Parliament. 'He was indeed made up of two men – a witty, well-read scholar, who wrote, disputed, and harangued, and a nervous, drivelling idiot who acted.'

James I and Queen Anne. The King admired the Queen, despite her intense extravagance, but his homosexual tendencies increased the breach between them, as did her Catholic sympathies as opposed to his Presbyterian upbringing.

existence. Having failed to persuade Somerset to procure for him the position of Ambassador to Venice, after the dissolution Donne wrote to his patron pointing out that he was 'now a year older, broken with some sore sickness', and begging for some hope of employment. All he received was the message, passed via Somerset from the King, that the Church was his best hope.

It was the last straw. After all, he gave up his hopes of secular preferment, and finally decided on Holy Orders – though not until he had travelled to Newmarket to see the King, and received re-assurance from him: 'as good allowance and encouragement to pursue my purpose as I could desire'. Magnanimously (for she particularly disliked Somerset, and Donne was still, if not directly in his employment, at least serving him) Lady Bedford offered to pay off all his debts, though she was able eventually to give him only £30 towards them, finding herself in some financial difficulty. Donne was very disappointed, and perhaps the Countess's inability to help him further prompted his decision to print a collection of his poems which would include not only some of his poems to her, but to other ladies, and which would be dedicated to Somerset. Such a book was never published, which was as well considering the disgrace shortly to fall on Somerset and his wife.

One more misfortune was to occur to Donne before he entered the Church: the death of his seven-year-old son Francis, who was buried in St Clement Danes in November 1614. Two months later, Donne was ordained by the Bishop of London. 'Now he had a new calling,' Walton puts it; 'new thoughts, and a new employment for his wit and eloquence. Now all his earthly affections were changed into divine love, and all the faculties of his own soul were engaged in the conversion of others, in preaching the glad tidings of remission to repenting sinners, and peace to each troubled soul.'

One of his first actions after his ordination was to go again to Newmarket to show himself to the King, who almost immediately appointed him Chaplain-in-Ordinary – a position which brought with it the right to two benefices, in addition to any other parish to which he might be appointed. His first official appearance with the King was at Cambridge on 7 March 1615 when he was at the centre of a dispute, for James wished his Chaplain to receive the University's honorary degree, and the University declined to bestow it. Donne's reputation as an erotic poet, together perhaps with recollections of the 'irregularities' he himself had confessed, and perhaps some

The Orthodox true Minister,   the Seducer and false Prophet.

'Who but myself can conceive the sweetness of that salutation, when the Spirit of God says to me in a morning, "Go forth today and preach; and preach consolation, preach peace, preach mercy."' Not all sermons were so well received by the Church as Donne's, as the portrayal of 'the Seducer and false Prophet' (*right*) indicates.

suspicion of Catholic leanings, made many men doubtful about him and his motives. However, he did receive an honorary degree very soon after the King had left Cambridge.

Donne is known to posterity in two roles: as poet and as preacher. He was a poet until the day of his death. It was now, by necessity, that his career as a preacher began – but began tentatively. Though as author of *Pseudo-Martyr* he could have commanded any pulpit in the land, and no doubt have drawn a large congregation, he seems to have preached at first in small and even out-of-the-way churches: at St Catherine's, Paddington, at Camberwell, and at the parish church at Greenwich. He preached at Court first in April 1616 and was to be a regular preacher at Whitehall until the end of his life. While he did not change from layman to complete clergyman in a moment, in the twinkling of an eye, his new solemnity must have offered him some protection from the tongues of slanderers when, in 1615, the Earl and Countess of Somerset were arrested for causing the death of Sir Thomas Overbury in the Tower. They were found guilty, and disgraced, though not executed. Donne was not dragged into the trial, but it is difficult to believe that he cannot have been in danger of a summons, for he must have known much of Somerset's private business.

He seems to have spent the first years of his life in the Church carefully cultivating his powers as a preacher. Walton gives a sketch of the way he spent his week:

As he usually preached once a week, if not oftener, so after his Sermon he never gave his eyes rest, till he had chosen out a new Text, and that night cast his Sermon into a form, and his Text into divisions; and the next day betook himself to consult the Fathers, and so commit his meditations to his memory, which was excellent. But upon Saturday he usually gave himself and his mind a rest from the weary burdens of his week's meditations, and usually spent that day in visitation of friends, or some other diversions of his thoughts; and would say that he gave both his body and mind that refreshment, that he might be enabled to do the work of the day following not faintly, but with courage and cheerfulness.

He certainly was not unduly detained by the cares of parishioners: though he accepted two benefices – the rectory of Keyston in Huntingdon, and of Sevenoaks in Kent – he never lived in either parish, where the vicars looked after the people while Donne enjoyed an income. (He is not too much to be blamed: pluralism was common in the seventeenth century, and he did at least visit the parishes from time to time.) In the autumn of 1616, he was chosen divinity reader of Lincoln's Inn, at a salary of £60 a year, together with accommodation, and dinner at the Bench's table. In return, he would preach fifty sermons a year.

Donne in 1616. A miniature by Isaac Oliver.

One imagines that he enjoyed this task. His congregations at Lincoln's Inn were intelligent men of his own type; there was little danger of complaints such as that made by one churchgoer, that 'he had too much learning in his sermon for ignoramuses'. The men of Lincoln's Inn were familiar with Donne's career, had probably read his manuscript poems (regretting this, he was to say later that 'their sin, that shall sin by occasion of any wanton writings of mine, will be my sin, though they come after'); and he was still sufficiently of their temperament to be able to forecast their reactions to his sermons. Even in later years, when he was relatively old, he remembered enough of his own youth to be able to engage the attention of a youthful gathering:

An old man wonders then how an arrow from an eye could wound him when he was young, and how Jove could make him do those things which he did then. And an arrow from the tongue of inferior people, that which we make shift to call honour, wounds him deeper now; and ambition makes him do strange things now as love did then. A fair day shoots arrows of visits, and comedies, and conversation, and so we go abroad; and a foul day shoots arrows of gaming, or chambering, and wantonness, and so we stay at home.

And again, 'Chastity is not chastity in an old man, but a disability to be unchaste.' Such sympathy was by no means apparent in the average parson. Nor was the shortening of a sermon so that the congregation could 'walk with God in the cool of the evening' of a summer's day.

Donne's technique as a preacher embraced the delivery as well as the composition of his sermons. He evidently had something like the *hwyll* of the Welsh Nonconformist preachers, 'weeping sometimes for his auditory, sometimes with them', as Walton put it; 'always preaching to himself, like an angel from a cloud, but in none; carrying some, as St Paul was, to Heaven in holy raptures, and enticing others by a sacred art and courtship to amend their lives; here picturing a vice so as to make it ugly to those that practised it, and a virtue so as to make it beloved, even by those that loved it not – and all this with a most particular grace, and an unexpressible addition of comeliness....'

Donne was fortunate in being able to deliver his first notable series of sermons to a congregation of intellectuals and wits. He was able to employ conceits, to put forward intellectual concepts, to use humour in ways which would have been less suitable for a large general congregation, as it would have been unsuitable in remote Paddington or distant Sevenoaks. In one of his earliest Lincoln's Inn sermons, for instance, he was able to enjoy a little speculation on the attentiveness of his listeners (surely never really in question), and to put it in such a manner that it might have been a prose version of one of his occasional poems:

I am not all here: I am here now preaching upon this text, and I am at home in my Library considering whether St Gregory, or St Jerome, have said best of this text before. I am here speaking to you: and yet I consider by the way, in the same instant, what it is likely you will say to one another when I have done. You are not all here, neither. You are here now, hearing me – and yet you are thinking that you have heard a better sermon somewhere else, of this text before. You are here, and yet you think you could have heard some other doctrine of downright predestination and reprobation roundly delivered somewhere else, with more edification to you. You are here, and you remember yourselves now ye think of it, this had been the fittest time, now, when everybody else is at Church, to have made such-and-such a private visit – and because you would be *there*, you *are* there!

The sermons were long, though not inordinately so. Congregations suffered much, in the seventeenth century, from wordy preachers. A villager giving evidence before an archdeacon's Court against a rector of Shawell in 1637 complained that

with a long extemporary prayer before and another very long prayer after them, many sermons have been ended so late in the evening that some of the parishioners have called for candle and lantern to go home by, and the young people and others of the said parish church have been thereby debarred of their lawful recreations graciously allowed them by his Majesty, and of sufficient and convenient fothering [feeding] of their cattle and doing of other business of necessity.

Donne did not inflict such cramping boredom on his hearers.

During the first months at Lincoln's Inn, Donne preached his most important early sermon. On the occasion of the anniversary of the death of Queen Elizabeth and the accession of James, the latter commanded him to preach from the open-air pulpit at the north-east corner of St Paul's Cathedral. Apart perhaps from some of the large gatherings at Speakers' Corner, there has never been since Tudor times an outdoor audience like the one that regularly assembled at Paul's Cross: all sorts of men from beggars to lords, and sometimes the King himself, came to hear the sermons, which were usually important, were often printed for circulation afterwards, and on some topic of the hour – so that at moments of national crisis a congregation would meet at the Cross to hear what was regarded as the 'official' Church of England view, and therefore to some extent the view of the government.

Donne, on that March day in 1617, distinguished himself before a large congregation, which included the Archbishop of Canterbury, the Lord Keeper, the Lord Privy Seal, several Earls and 'divers other great men'. A contemporary reports that he preached 'a dainty sermon . . . exceedingly well liked generally, the rather for that he did Queen Elizabeth great right, and held himself close to the text without flattering the time too much.'

He recalled vividly the traumatic shock of the death of the Queen, who had reigned so long and with such distinction that she seemed England itself:

Every one of you in the city were running up and down like ants with their eggs bigger than themselves, every man with his bags, to seek where to hide them safely. . . . In the death of that Queen, unmatchable, inimitable in her sex; that Queen, worthy, I will not say of Nestor's years, I will not say of Methusalem's, but worthy of Adam's years, if Adam had never fallen; in her death we were all under one common flood, and depth of tears.

Donne's greeting to King James was unelaborate, even equivocal: 'When men may speak freely of the virtues of a dead Prince, it is an evident argument that the present Prince practises the same virtues; for if he did not, he would not love to hear of them.'

Burials

August

Elizabeth Seares D of Samuel	2
John Binnion S of Reignold	3
John Knifton S of William	7
Mary Sanders, wife of William	8
John Pelton, Housholder	
Rogers	9
Sarah Betty D of Henry	
Anne Bell D of Thomas	10
Margaret Willmut D of Edward	12
Bennet Snow D of John	14
Elizabeth Atkins D of John	
Alice Reignolds D of Roger	15
Mrs Anne Dun, wife of Dr Dun	16
Leonard Fort S of Humphry	17
John Adams, seruant wth Mr Barksted	18
John Stony-brasse S of John	
Barbara Peircy, Seruant wth John Porter	21
Joan Ratcold, wife of Richard	23
Elizabeth Rogers, wife of Thomas	
Elizabeth Fisher D of William	25
Anne Lee, D of Richard	

Later that year, Donne was to face the second great emotional crisis of his life. The first had been when he married Ann. The second was when, in August, she gave birth to a stillborn child, and a week later died. The records of St Clement Danes tell the story. On 16 August appear a few sad lines:

> For the burial of a stillborn child of Dr Donne's:
>   for the grave in the church 4s
>   for the knell 8d
> For the burial of Mrs Donne:
>   for the knell 5s
>   for the passing bell 4d

Bells continually tolled out the deaths of London's citizens. Fynes Moryson, travelling in England in 1617, noted that 'when any man

Entry 16 in the church register of St Clement Danes records the death of 'Mrs Anne Dun, wife of Dr Dun'.

(*Opposite*) Preaching in the open air at St Paul's Cross. 'All the sermon is not God's word, but all the sermon is God's ordinance, and the text is certainly his word. There is no salvation but by faith, nor faith but by hearing, nor hearing but by preaching.'

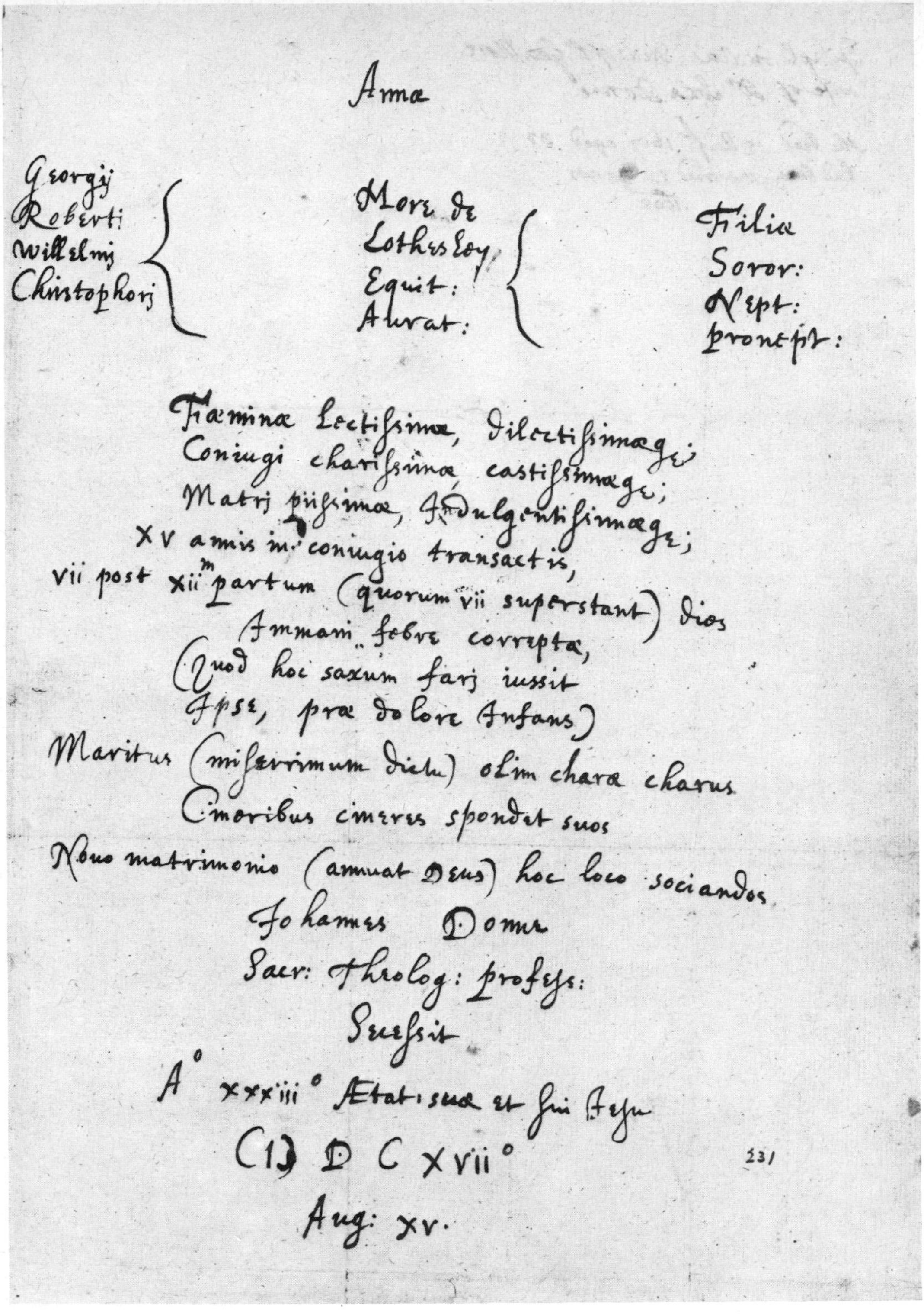

Annæ

Georgij
Roberti
Willelmij
Christophorj

More de
Lothesley
Equit:
Aurat:

Filiæ
Soror:
Nept:
Proneptj:

Fæminæ Lectissimæ, dilectissimæq;
Coniugi charissimæ castissimæq;
Matrj piissimæ, & indulgentissimæq;
XV annis in coniugio transactis,
vii post xii^m partum (quorum vii superstant) dies
Annam febre correpta,
(Quod hoc saxum farj iussit
Ipse, præ dolore Infans)
Maritus (miserrimum dictu) olim chara charus
Cineribus cineres spondet suos

Novo matrimonio (annuat Deus) hoc loco sociandos.
Johannes Donne
Sacr: Theolog: profess:
Prefsit
A° xxxiii° Ætatis suæ et Jïi Jesu
(I) D C Xvii°

231

Aug: Xv.

is at the point of death, a great bell is tolled to warn all men to pray for him while he yet liveth; and when the party is dead by a number of several strokes at the bell notice is given whether the party dead be a man, woman or child, and then the bell is rung out. As likewise at the burial the bells of the church for some hours are rung out.' Here are the knells, the passing bells.

Later, 'a little tomb in a wall' was set up in memory of Ann, carved by Nicholas Stone, who had made the monument for the grave of Sir Robert Drury a while before. Mother and child lay in one grave.

A few days after his wife's burial, Donne preached a sermon in St Clement's on the text from Jeremiah: 'Lo, I am the man that have seen affliction.'

And indeed [Walton says] his very words and looks testified him to be truly such a man; and they, with the addition of his sighs and tears, expressed in his Sermon, did so work upon the affections of his hearers, as melted and moulded them into a companionable sadness; and so they left the Congregation; but then their houses presented them with objects of diversion: and his presented him with nothing but fresh objects of sorrow, in beholding many helpless children, a narrow fortune, and a consideration of the many cares and casualties that attended their education.

Of Ann's twelve children, seven still lived: Constance, the eldest, was fourteen years old, and Elizabeth, the youngest, just twelve months. Their sorrow augmented Donne's own, which was profound. It was one thing to preach the joy of reunion in heaven, to write of God winning Ann's soul from him by the offer of a heavenly love; quite another to accept phlegmatically the death of a relatively young woman to whom, though through great love, her husband had brought little but a life of relative poverty and drudgery, incessant childbearing and consequent illness.

Every student of Donne's surviving sermons, and indeed of his divine poems, has remarked on the increased depth of his religious feeling after Ann's death. None has put it more vividly than Walton: after Ann died, Donne

became crucified to the world, and all those vanities, those imaginary pleasures that are daily acted on that restless stage; and they were as perfectly crucified to him. Nor is it hard to think – being, passions may be both changed and heightened by accidents – but that abundant affection which once was between him and her who had long been the delight of his eyes and the companion of his youth; her, with whom he had divided so many pleasant sorrows and contented fears as common people are not capable of; – not hard to think but that she being now removed by death, a commensurable grief took as full as possession of him as joy had done; and so indeed it did, for now his soul was elemented of nothing but sadness; now grief took so full a possession of his heart as to leave no place for joy.

Donne's draft of his epitaph for his wife, 'Annae', which Nicholas Stone inscribed on her monument, 'in the Chancel, on the north side, at the upper end' of St Clement Danes Church.

Lincoln's Inn Chapel. Donne helped to plan the building of this chapel, at which he preached an inaugural sermon on 22 May 1623.

It would be silly to suppose that Donne had never before considered the most profound implications of the Christian faith: had never pondered the terrible problem of the reconciliation of the idea of a loving God with the facts of sickness and pain, the death of a loved and loving wife. But his reflections now became more profound, more immediate, and the expression of his conclusions in prose and verse more moving and more steadfast.

For some time his friends feared for his health, and even for his life, so much was he affected by Ann's death. But very gradually he began to recover his balance: began preaching regularly once more, took an interest in the new chapel planned by the Benchers of Lincoln's Inn, and renewed contacts with some of his old friends. In the early spring of 1619, he was given an opportunity to travel. Viscount Doncaster (formerly James Hay) was to be sent to mediate between the Bohemians (troubled at the suppression of their Protestant elements) and the Emperor Matthias of Germany who, supported as head of the Habsburg Confederation by Spain, saw the Bohemian protests as a simple act of Protestant defiance of a Catholic monarch. The King appointed Donne as Doncaster's chaplain.

Donne was not at all eager to go abroad, 'to leave a scattered flock of wretched children', as he wrote to Goodyer, 'to carry an infirm and valetudinary body, and go into the mouth of such adversaries as I cannot blame for hating me, the Jesuits'. He was still ill and depressed, and preoccupied with death. While he was sorting out his papers and making arrangements for his departure, came the news of the death of Queen Anne, and then of the serious illness of the King; and when Donne preached on Easter Day, his were sombre and telling words, in perhaps the earliest of his truly great sermons:

All our life is but a going out to the place of execution, to death. Now was there ever any man seen to sleep in the cart between Newgate and Tyburn? Between the prison and the place of execution, does any man sleep? And we sleep all the way; from the womb to the grave we are never thoroughly awake; but pass on with such dreams, and imaginations as these, 'I may live as well as another'; and 'Why should *I* die, rather than another?' But awake, and tell me, says this text, '*Quis homo?* Who is that other that thou talkest of? What man is he that liveth, and shall not see death?'

He became more worried as his departure approached (one must remember the difficulties and dangers of a journey into Europe in the seventeenth century, and at a time of unrest at the beginning of the Thirty Years War). He wrote a poem, *A Hymn to Christ, at the Author's last going into Germany*, which was in reality a preparation for possible death during the enterprise: the poem was a 'bill of my divorce to all', speaks of sailing in a 'torn ship' and of the sea swallowing him in a flood, and looks to the possibility that he might escape the storms of travel only in 'an everlasting night'.

On 18 April, at Lincoln's Inn, he preached a farewell sermon to his congregation, inviting his friends to remember him, as he did them. It is of course always a sermon: 'remember my labours and endeavours, at least my desire, to make sure your salvation, and I shall remember your religious cheerfulness in hearing the word, and your Christianly respect towards all them that bring that word unto you, and towards myself in particular, far above my merit.' Yet there is a touch almost of the lover bidding farewell to his mistress: 'And so as your eyes that stay here, and mine that must be far off, for all that distance shall meet every morning in looking upon the same sun, and meet every night in looking upon the same moon; so our hearts may meet morning and evening in that God which sees and hears everywhere. . . .' It was to be a familiar touch in his sermons, which however noble their language or convoluted their imagery or theological argument, remained always at some level in touch with the simple workings of the human heart.

Heidelberg (*above*), Munich, Salzburg and Frankfurt (*opposite, top to bottom*). 'Remember me thus, you that stay in this kingdom of peace, where no sword is drawn but the sword of Justice, as I shall remember you in those kingdoms where ambition on one side and a necessary defence from unjust persecution on the other side hath drawn many swords.'

It is a melancholy sermon, so positive a farewell that we cannot doubt that Donne was convinced he would never return. He spoke in the same terms to his friends: he was going 'out of the Kingdom, and perchance out of the world'. He was obviously in the middle of a deep depression, not only to be accounted for by the death, two years earlier, of Ann, or by having to leave his children. But he had to go, and early in May a sombrely dressed company of courtiers rode out of London in over twenty-five carriages, in mourning for their Queen, but no doubt spirited enough to begin already to divert their chaplain from his uneasiness. The company landed at Calais on 12 May.

This visit to Europe, which was to last for seven months, did Donne nothing but good. It was, more or less, a holiday – though of course he had certain duties, such as taking prayers regularly for the Viscount and the members of his party, and occasionally preaching to a larger congregation (before the Elector Palatine at Heidelberg, for instance, and those of that household who spoke English). Doncaster had a delicate mission, and it seems that he was no match for the superior politics of the men with whom he had to deal. He accomplished little if anything, and succeeded only in infuriating the Spaniards, who on his return to England accused him of taking Bohemia's part.

There was a constant change of scene: Brussels, Cologne, and by river to Frankfurt; Heidelberg, Stuttgart, Ulm, Munich (where the party stayed at the ducal palace, which Doncaster found 'second to none in Europe'); then to Salzburg, to Cologne, and back to Aix-la-Chapelle. From Maastricht, the next stop, Doncaster wrote to Lincoln's Inn to apologize on Donne's behalf for his not being present there for the beginning of the Michaelmas term: 'I shall receive it for a singular favour from you, that you would so long spare to me from yourselves a person so necessary to you, and so agreeable to me. I hope to restore him to you by the midst of Michaelmas term.'

From Maastricht, Doncaster and his train went to Cologne, and then once more embarked on the Rhine for Frankfurt, where during a short delay – the party spent much time waiting about for various notabilities who Doncaster always seemed to contrive to miss – they shed their mourning for the Queen and, with money lent by Doncaster

Ferdinand II, whose early education
by the Jesuits imbued him with a
deep hatred of Protestantism.

The medal commemorating the
Synod of Dort.

himself, bought new and more colourful clothes. By the end of
September, Doncaster and most of his party (including Donne) were
on the way to Nuremberg, called at Vienna, and finally arrived at
Graz, where the new Emperor Ferdinand of Styria received them in
audience. Donne was much impressed by Ferdinand, and recalled
some years later in a sermon how 'even at the audience of an ambassador, at the sound of a bell he knelt down in our presence and prayed'.

His audience with the Holy Roman Emperor completed Doncaster's mission, and he decided to turn south for a visit to Venice.
But the Venetians had imposed a quarantine for fear of plague, and
reluctantly the party turned back through Vienna and Graz, through
Nuremberg, Worms and Heidelberg, sailed down-river to Arnhem,
and made a courtesy call at The Hague. Here Donne was among
those members of the train to be presented with a gold medal struck to
commemorate the Synod of Dort, that last stand of rigid Calvinism,

when the Dutch Reformed Church decided the theological differences between the Calvinists and Arminians by declining to hear the
latter's arguments. At The Hague, too, he preached.

On 1 January 1620 Doncaster's party rode into London, Donne
'with his sorrows moderated, and his health improved', according to
Walton. Within a week, he was preaching again at Lincoln's Inn,
and although he took up in his earliest sermons the old theme of death
and decay, it was in altogether a different spirit – concentrating on the
resurrection rather than the body's decay.

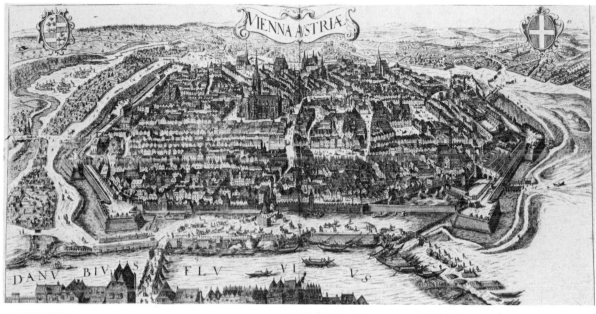

(*Above*) Vienna, where Doncaster
appeared 'con pompa grande', and
was received by the Archduke of
Austria.

(*Left*) The Hague, where Donne
preached two sermons – one on the
sin of Pride.

In somewhat better spirits than he had been since Ann's death, Donne must have felt confident that his career in the Church was now secure. He oversaw the religious conduct of the members of Lincoln's Inn, felt that he had confirmed his friendship with Doncaster, and confidently expected promotion when the death of a senior church-man should make that possible. In March, when the Bishop of Salisbury died, he may have hoped for a deanery there, but was disappointed. In 1621, the Bishop of London died, and there were again rumours that Donne would go to Salisbury, when that Dean came to London, to Westminster; other rumours gave him the deanery at Gloucester, but yet again they were unfounded. Donne had not shaken off the old habit of rushing in whenever a promotion seemed possible, and there exists a letter from him to the Duke of Buckingham complaining that it was not realized 'how narrow and penurious a fortune I wrestle with in this world', and in language which now seems immoderately humble, assuring the Duke that 'I lie in a corner as a clod of clay, attending what kind of vessel it shall please you to make of your Lordship's humblest and thankfulest and devotedest servant. . . .'

Life cannot have been as poor or as drab as that letter suggests: Donne was living a placid and far from unhappy life, looked after (at least from time to time) by his eldest daughter Constance, enjoying his close association with the members of Lincoln's Inn, writing regularly to Goodyer and other friends, troubled only by an attack of writer's cramp which made it difficult for him to copy out his sermons.

Late in August, promotion at last came: he was appointed Dean of St Paul's. Walton claims that James himself broke the news:

The King sent to Dr Donne, and appointed him to attend him at Dinner. . . . When his Majesty was sat down, before he had eat any meat, he said after his pleasant manner, 'Dr Donne, I have invited you to dinner; and, though you sit not down with me, yet I will carve to you of a dish that I know you love well; for knowing you love London, I do therefore make you Dean of Paul's; and when I have dined, then do you take your beloved dish home to your study; say grace there to yourself, and much good may it do you.'

The story has been disputed: if true, the news must have compensated even for such a distressing sight as that of James I at table, 'his tongue too large for his mouth, which ever made him speak full in the mouth, and made him drink very uncomely, as if eating his drink, which came out into the cup on each side of his mouth'.

Donne could scarcely have hoped for anything better than his new appointment. Certainly, the achievement was not for want of trying. He had cultivated for many years almost every notable man who was likely to be able to forward his career, at first out of the Church, and latterly in it. If his assiduous courtships – 'toadyings', one commentator

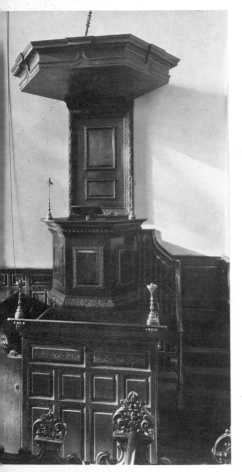

The pulpit of Lincoln's Inn Chapel. 'Every master of a family . . . when he comes to kneel at the side of his table to pray, he comes to build a church there, and therefore should sanctify that place.'

James I. 'He was of a middle stature, more corpulent through his clothes than in his body, yet fat enough. . . . His legs were very weak, that weakness made him ever leaning on other men's shoulders. His walk was ever circular.'

has said – are somewhat unpleasant to a twentieth-century mind, one must remember that the payment of flowery compliments was much more common then than now, that the gaining of promotion was far from dependent on merit alone, and that worse men had employed less honest means than Donne to gain positions of prestige or power.

On Thursday afternoon, 22 November 1621, Donne waited in a house near St Paul's while the Chapter of the Cathedral met to hear the official letter from the King commanding Donne's election as

Old St Paul's: the nave.

(*Opposite*) Donne in 1620, aged forty-eight: the portrait in the Deanery of St Paul's.

Dean. The members cast their votes; the result of the election was brought to the new Dean, and he was presented to the Bishop. Then, led in procession by the Bishop and canons, he entered the Cathedral and approached the high altar, where a solemn *Te Deum* was sung. He prostrated himself, rose, and was led to his seat in the choir and installed in it, swearing to live at the Cathedral, protect its rights and preserve its possessions. The canons swore obedience to him, and the new Dean himself swore obedience to the Bishop.

While he received some new perquisites (becoming, for instance, Prebendary of Chiswick), he had to give up his position at Lincoln's Inn (receiving as a gift from the Benchers the fine edition of the Vulgate Bible still to be seen at the Library there). In an official minute, the Benchers hoped that their old friend might 'at his pleasure and convenient leisure repair to this house, being a worthy member thereof, and be no stranger here', and that he should 'continue his Chamber in this house which he now hath, as a Bencher of this house with such privileges touching the same as the Masters of the Bench now have and ought to have . . . .'.

One special occasion took Donne back to Lincoln's Inn as preacher: this was the consecration of the new chapel, for the building of which he had been an assiduous champion. A huge congregation crowded into the building. Donne's contemporary, John Chamberlain, recorded the occasion: 'There was great concourse of noblemen and gentlemen whereof two or three were endangered and taken up dead for the time with the extreme press and thronging. . . .' Although he would certainly have kept in touch with his friends there, this was virtually Donne's last connection with Lincoln's Inn: he finally left his chambers in November 1624.

The new Dean of St Paul's was (as the portrait of 1620 shows) an imposing figure, quite apart from his growing reputation as a preacher. He was eminently suited to his office. As Walton wrote:

His fancy was inimitably high, equalled only by his great wit, both being made useful by a commanding judgement. His aspect was cheerful, and such as gave a silent testimony of a clear, knowing soul, and of a conscience at peace with itself. His melting eye showed that he had a soft heart, full of noble compassion; of too brave a soul to offer injuries, and too much a Christian not to pardon them in others. . . .

His position was no sinecure, and he could certainly not have relied solely on personality or on his power as a preacher to maintain it. He had to oversee the work of five archdeacons, a precentor (responsible for running the services of the Cathedral), a treasurer and a chancellor, four resident canons, twelve minor canons, six vicars choral (the 'singing men' who, with the choirboys, led the singing at services), and finally the men who looked after the non-religious aspects of the

ST PAVLES CHVRCH

Old St Paul's, from the Thames, in 1616. The church was to be completely destroyed in the Great Fire of 1666.

building itself – such as the vergers who were constantly on duty, but who seem at this time to have done very little to maintain the decencies.

The problem was that every Londoner regarded St Paul's as a convenient and proper place to meet and do business: it was in the middle of the very busiest area of the city, crowded with street traders, noisy with the rumble of wooden-wheeled carts bringing goods in from the country to sell, with porters carrying wares unloaded from ships at the city wharves and often using the Cathedral as a handy short-cut to the warehouses in the north of London. Thomas Dekker described it as a marvellous meeting-place where 'the main shoal of islanders are swimming up and down'. Young men stood hatted in the aisles in front of pillars covered with advertisements, waiting for employment; behind the same pillars waited the choirboys to claim 'spur money' from any young hotblood who walked in wearing spurs.

The church was noisier even than it is today; and the tourists of the 1620s were less considerate – they climbed up to carve their names in the leaded roof, 'which already contains more names than Stow's *Chronicle*'; they would frequently urinate behind the pillars, and in the afternoon 'the boys and maids and children of the adjoining parishes . . . after dinner come into church and play as children used to till dark night'.

Donne seems to have found the situation quite beyond him: there were a few prosecutions, and at least once he spoke a few sharp words from the pulpit ('There come some persons to this Church of whom I never saw master nor servant kneel at his coming into Church, or at any part of divine service.') But the custom was too well established for the most rigorous Dean or the most lively vergers to arrest it.

Donne's duties as regards the business of the Cathedral were much more adequately performed. They needed some skill. There was the matter, for instance, of the Chapter's patronage (no one can say that Donne had not had experience of seeking and sometimes obtaining patronage, in the past). The Chapter had livings in its gift, and Donne was for the most part solely responsible for administering them – which he did wisely and without, as far as we can tell, ever receiving a gift in respect of a single one. An uncommon pheno-menon. Then he was concerned with the Cathedral's income from rents and the disposal of leases. The fact that he had for some years himself to be extremely careful of the disposition of his own small income may account for the scrupulous care with which he saw that the Cathedral's records were kept, and its money spent.

As far as religious duties went, he was only bound to preach at St Paul's on three days in the year: Christmas Day, Easter Day and Ascension Day. In fact, he preached much more often, mounting the pulpit without notes, and preaching with great grace and a perfect command of language. His congregations wondered at this, perhaps not realizing the extent to which he prepared his sermons, writing them out in full on important occasions and learning them by heart. He had been known as a preacher hitherto: now he became really renowned, with the authority of his position to give his words addi-tional solemnity, and with wide experience of various congregations to help him gauge his delivery of them.

The sermons he preached at St Paul's have all survived, and often been reprinted. In them, he achieves a singular magnificence of expression. While he may later have revised some of them, they must have sounded from the pulpit like the utterances of a divine spirit. One or two passages have become properly famous. If one might quote one example, it should perhaps be the superb central section of the sermon on *God's Mercies* preached at St Paul's on Christmas Day 1624 (in this instance I preserve the punctuation and spelling of the original):

God made Sun and Moon to distinguish seasons, and day, and night, and we cannot have the fruits of the earth but in their seasons: But God hath made no decree to distinguish the seasons of his mercies; In paradise, the fruits were ripe, the first minute, and in heaven it is alwaies Autumne, his mercies are ever in their maturity. We ask *panem quotidianum*, our daily bread, and God never sayes you should have come yesterday, he never sayes you must againe to morrow, but *to day if you will heare his voice*, to day he will heare you. If some King of the earth have so large an extent of Dominion, in North,

Bee Wise as serpents but inosent as Dous.

LXXX.
SERMONS
PREACHED BY THAT LEAR.
NED AND REVEREND DIVINE
IOHN DONNE D.ᴿ IN DIVINITIE
LATE DEANE OF yᵗ CATHEDRALL
CHVRCH OF Sᵗ PAVLES
LONDON.

M.Merian Iun:

(*Left*) The Church of St Edmund, Blunham, with (*above*) the base of the chalice presented by Donne, inscribed with his name.

and South, as that he hath Winter and Summer together in his Dominions, so large an extent East and West, as that he hath day and night together in his Dominions, much more hath God mercy and judgement together: He brought light out of darknesse, not out of a lesser light; he can bring thy Summer out of Winter, though thou have no Spring; though in the wayes of fortune, or understanding, or conscience, thou have been benighted till now, wintred and frozen, clouded and eclypsed, damped and benummed, smothered and stupified till now, now God comes to thee, not as in the dawning of the day, not as in the bud of the spring, but as the Sun at noon to illustrate all shadowes, as the sheaves in harvest, to fill all penuries, all occasions invite his mercies, and all times are his seasons.

Small wonder that crowds pressed into St Paul's to hear such words.

Business outside the walls of the Cathedral pressed upon the Dean. Some of it was a direct result of his appointment. He became Rector of Blunham, in Bedfordshire, for instance (again, a local curate took care of the parish, though Donne visited it from time to time, and gave the church a silver-gilt chalice). His position as Dean brought non-ecclesiastical work, too – he became a Justice of the Peace for Kent and

(*Opposite*) *LXXX Sermons* was published by command of Charles I, in 1640. The book was edited by Donne's eldest son, John, from the original manuscripts. The sermon on *God's Mercies* was *Sermon II* in this edition.

Bedford in the 1620s, and was appointed more or less regularly to hear appeals from ecclesiastical courts. His legal knowledge, spasmodically and somewhat painfully acquired during those early months at the Inns of Court, was now extremely useful.

There were other less onerous duties, such as the governorship of Charterhouse (Sutton's Hospital). He regarded none of them as simply honorary – the records show for instance that he attended all the meetings of the Charterhouse governors between 1626 and 1631, and his signature appears at the foot of the minutes.

Such work carried no income, but the Deanery had placed him well out of his financial worries. Dr R. C. Bald has estimated that his total income must have been over £2000 a year in the currency of the 1620s. He lived with his family, at the Deanery – a comfortable house with a sizeable garden. He was able to invite his ageing mother to live with him. There must have been those who muttered at the presence at the Deanery of a woman several times prosecuted for papist leanings; but Donne loved her, and wanted her with him. He has sometimes been accused of stony-heartedness after Ann's death; his treatment of his mother belies it. The few records of his filial feelings show their depth. In 1616, for instance, hearing of the death of Anne Lyly, his sister, he had written his mother a long letter of sympathy and love:

For my part, which am only left now to do the office of a child, though the poorness of my fortune and the greatness of my charge hath not suffered me to express my duty towards you as became me, yet I protest to you before Almighty God and his Angels and Saints in Heaven that I do and ever shall esteem myself to be as strongly bound to look to you and provide for your relief as for my own poor wife and children. For whatsoever I shall be able to do, I acknowledge to be a debt to you, from whom I had that education which must make my fortune. . . .

Now, he was able to repay that debt.

In his new affluence, he showed a generous disposition; he sent £100 to an old friend 'whom he had known live plentifully, and by a too liberal heart and carelessness become decayed in his estate' (Dr Bald conjectures this to have been Goodyer); Walton records that he freed many prisoners who were in gaol for debt, gave freely to students, and regularly sent a servant to the London prisons on festival days, to distribute gifts.

Now that Donne was at last in a position of authority in the Church, he found it no longer possible to be reticent about matters of national concern: he was expected to support the establishment, and one discovers him doing so fairly early in his time as Dean. In the autumn of 1622, he preached at Paul's Cross a sermon in support of the King's *Direction to Preachers*, issued to control the topics about which the clergy might speak from their pulpits. The release of certain imprisoned English Catholics (with which James had shown his goodwill towards Spain, hoping to speed up the proposed alliance between the Prince of Wales and a Spanish bride) had led to some concern, and the King, hoping to stop the muttered discontent from swelling, now laid it down that the clergy should preach only about the subjects covered in the Thirty-Nine Articles and the Book of Homilies, and that on Sunday afternoons they should not preach at all. There should be no attempt on their part 'to meddle with matters of state and the differences between prince and people', and 'no railing against either papists or puritans'.

Donne's support of the King's move was not on the whole very satisfactory; one listener said that he spoke 'as if himself were not so well satisfied'. But James was happy: he read Donne's sermon, and found it 'a piece of such perfection as could admit neither addition nor diminution'. He commanded that it should be printed, and it became, unworthily, the first of Donne's sermons to be published.

On other occasions, the Dean spoke with more enthusiasm and to better effect. He delivered, in November 1622, what has been called the first missionary sermon to be preached in England. He had been made a member of the Virginia Company, and an honorary member of its council. Four hundred people gathered at St Martin's, Cornhill, to hear a distinguished sermon in which Donne enjoined the Company to see that the Gospel should be preached to the natives of the countries now being opened up to trade. He was under no illusion about the main purposes of exploratory settlements – apart from anything else, they disposed of unwanted criminals, who made ideal settlers. The settlements should 'sweep your streets, and wash your doors from idle persons, and the children of idle persons, and employ them; and truly, if the whole country were but such a Bridewell, to force idle persons to work, it had a good use.'

Then, of course, there was trade: 'already the place gives essays, nay freights of merchantable commodities', though the Dean deplored the fact that religious motives were not also consulted: 'O, if you would be as ready to hearken at the return of a ship how many Indians were converted to Christ Jesus, as what trees or drugs or dyes that ship had brought, then you were in your right way, and not till then.'

The congregation, no doubt properly impressed, trooped out of church into the Merchant Taylors' Hall to sit down to a dinner of venison, for which they had paid three shillings a head.

The relief of Donne's financial difficulties left him still with a few problems, one of which was the finding of husbands for his two elder daughters – Constance was now almost twenty, Bridget fourteen. Donne, while now in command of a pleasant enough income, could not possibly lay his hands on enough capital to allow them a sufficiently large dowry to catch a really substantial husband. While it was less costly to dispose of daughters than sons, dowries might run to between £1000 and £3000 for an ordinary squire; a baronet or minor peer would cost about £5000, and an earl as much as £10,000.

Donne, remembering the circumstances of his own marriage, might have permitted a marriage for love, but would scarcely have welcomed it. Fortunately, neither girl seemed husband-mad: he wrote to Goodyer (who faced much the same problem), 'I think they will not murmur if heaven must be their nunnery, and they associated with the blessed virgins there.'

He had got as far as entering into negotiations with at least one young man, but the arrangement had come to nothing. The story, as he tells it to Goodyer, provides an interesting insight into the customs of the age:

Tell both your daughters a piece of the story of my Con, which may accustom them to endure disappointments in this world. An honourable person . . . had an intention to give her one of his sons, and had told it to me, and would have been content to accept what I, by my friends, could have begged for her; but he intended that son to my profession, and had provided him already £300 a year of his own gift in church livings, and hath estated £300 more of inheritance for their children. And now the youth (who yet knows nothing of his father's intention nor mine) flies from his resolution for that calling, and importunes his father to let him travel. The girl knows not her loss, for I never told her of it; but truly it is a great disappointment to me.

The question of providing a husband for Constance continued to preoccupy the Dean, and in October 1623 he invited Sir Thomas Grymes (his brother-in-law) and the actor Edward Alleyn to dinner, to discuss the matter. Alleyn's wife had died a few months previously, and it is fairly obvious that he had his eye on Constance, and was supported by Grymes, who with his wife was particularly fond of the young woman.

Alleyn, now fifty-eight years old, had been an extraordinarily successful actor – 'a youth of excellent capacity, a cheerful temper, a tenacious memory, a sweet elocution, and in his person of a stately port and aspect', a contemporary said. It was considered at the time of the negotiations with the Dean that 'he could not be worth less than £25,000', and Dibdin says that his fortune had grown partly because of his success as an actor, 'partly from his being Keeper of the King's Wild Beasts, and Master of the Royal Bear Garden, and partly from his being a most rigid and penurious economist'.

Alleyn seems to have known Donne thirty years previously, though perhaps not well. After their dinner-party, he wrote a memorandum which he sent to the Dean. It reveals baldly the businesslike coldness of such contracts:

Edward Alleyn, actor, founder of
Dulwich College, and Donne's
son-in-law.

FIVE SERMONS VPON SPECIALL OCCASIONS.

(Viz.)

1. A Sermon preached at *Pauls* Croſſe.
2. To the Honorable the *Virginia* Company
3. At the Conſecration of *Lincolnes Inne* Chappell.
4. The firſt Sermon preached to K. *Charles* at St. *Iames,* 1625.
5. A Sermon preached to his Maieſtie at *White-hall,* 24. *Febr.* 1625.

By IOHN DONNE *Deane of Saint* Pauls, *London.*

LONDON,
Printed for THOMAS IONES, and are to bee
ſold at the Signe of the *Blacke Rauen* in the
Strand. 1626.

More of Donne's sermons survive for the year 1626 than for any other year; and five were also published during that year.

After motions made by Sir Thomas Grymes on both sides, I was invited to your house the 21 of October 1623, where after dinner in your parlour you declared your intention to bestow with your daughter Con all the benefits of your prime lease (which as you said you knew would shortly be renewed), and that you were assured if I stayed till Michaelmas next to be worth £500 at the least, and whensoever it should rise to more, it should wholly be hers. My offer was to do as much for her as yourself, and add to that at my death £500 more, and so her estate should be £1000.

This gave not content, and Sir Thomas persuaded me to do somewhat more, which I did, and promised to leave her at my death 2,000 marks [a mark, a term used only in accountancy, represented two-thirds of a pound]. This was accepted, and security demanded.

94

Constance was not kept in the dark about the plans being made for her future. Alleyn noted that 'I presently returned to Peckham, and coming then to Con, told her what had passed; and more, to show my love to her off my own voluntary, I told her before Sir Thomas I would make it up to £1500.'

The marriage took place early in December, in unwonted haste, for Donne had fallen seriously ill of an epidemic which was at large in London. He described the attack in the *Devotions upon Emergent Occasions and several steps in my Sickness*, which he wrote sitting up in his bedroom, as he slowly recovered.

This minute I was well, and am ill this minute. I am surprised with a sudden change, and alteration to worse, and can impute it to no cause, nor call it by any name. [He suffered from] sudden shakings; these lightnings, sudden flashes; these thunders, sudden noises; these eclipses, sudden offuscations and darkenings of [the] senses; these blazing stars, sudden fiery exhalations; these rivers of blood, sudden red waters. . . . In the twinkling of an eye, I can scarce see, instantly the taste is insipid and fatuous; instantly the appetite is dull and desireless; instantly the knees are sinking and strengthless; and in an instant sleep, which is the picture, the copy of death, is taken away, that the original, death itself, may succeed. . . .

The doctor is called:

I see he fears, and I fear with him – I overtake him, I overrun him in his fear, and I go the faster, because he makes his pace slow; I fear the more because he disguises his fear, and I see it with the more sharpness because he would not have me see it.

The strange remedies of Elizabethan and Jacobean medicine are applied: there are cordials, dead pigeons are placed at the feet 'to draw the vapours from the brain'. A rash of spots appears, and sleepless he lies listening to the tolling of the bells as those who have died in the same epidemic are carried to their funerals. One of the most famous of all Donne's prose passages springs from that moment:

No man is an island, entire of itself; every man is a piece of the continent, a part of the main. If a clod be washed away by the sea, Europe is the less, as well as if a promontory were, as well as if a manor of thy friend's or of thine own were. Any man's death diminishes me, because I am involved in mankind. And therefore never send to know for whom the bell tolls. It tolls for thee.

The illness, which has been diagnosed as relapsing fever, also prompted three poems: *A Hymn to God the Father*, *Hymn to God my God, in my sickness*, and the sonnet 'O to vex me, contraries meet in one'. The first, Walton tells us, was set to music

to a most grave and solemn tune, and to be often sung to the organ by the choristers of St Paul's Church, in his own hearing, especially at the evening service; and at his return from his customary devotions in that place, did occasionally say to a friend . . . 'O, the power of church-music! That harmony added to this hymn has raised the affections of my heart, and quickened my graces of zeal and gratitude; and I observe that I always return from paying this public duty of prayer and praise to God with an unexpressible tranquillity of mind, and a willingness to leave the world.'

The *Devotions* appeared in print (in February 1624) before Donne was out and about; he was not sufficiently recovered to preach the Lent sermon to the Court. But he appeared in the pulpit again on Easter Day, at St Paul's, and later in March received a new appointment as Vicar of St Dunstan's-in-the-West. This was no sinecure; indeed, the parish had been rather neglected by the former incumbent, an aged man, and Donne set about repairing the fabric of its pattern of worship. It was a city parish within Temple Bar, attended by many judges and other legal men, as well as a great number of fashionable citizens. Printers and stationers too found it a convenient church (many of the latter had their shops in the churchyard, including Marriott, who published Donne).

Donne preached his first sermon at St Dunstan's on 11 April. His care for that church was keen and lasting. In the first months he saw to the building of a new pulpit and new pews, and persuaded the members of Clifford's Inn (who had been using the church as their chapel, and crowding out the parishioners) to rebuild their pews so that they would not encroach too much on the rest of the congregation. His parishioners were properly grateful to him for his interest: one Christmas they sent him a gift of six gallons of sack and two sugar-loaves.

In 1625, Donne found himself involved in an undignified squabble with his son-in-law. Alleyn, who despite his fortune was constantly in need of money – he was the founder of Dulwich College and of various foundations which were a constant drain on his funds – suddenly applied to him for the loan of £500, and was refused. He was furious. Donne had, he said, placed a small sum of money 'before my honesty, your own reputation or your daughter's good'. Donne, not unnaturally, lost his temper, using (Alleyn said) 'words more fitting you thirty years ago when you might be questioned for them, than now under so reverend a calling as you are'.

The retired actor wrote a long and vituperative letter in which accusation followed accusation: Donne had never sent to Constance that linen of her mother's which had been promised them; he had purposely sent away to his son John at Oxford a horse which he knew Con wanted for herself; he had persuaded Con to give him her diamond ring by promising to exchange it for a better, but had never done so; he had told Alleyn a lease he had given him was worth £500 when in fact he was getting £550 from it, and pocketing the extra £50; Alleyn had always been told he would be welcome at the

Deanery, but whenever he wanted to stay there was always informed that it was inconvenient; and finally Con's sister Lucy had been living with the Alleyns' for rather too long, and Donne was 'better able to bear her charge'.

Both men were 'careful' about money: Donne, because of the years of struggle when he had barely enough to live on. As far as finance was concerned, it cannot have been easy for them to get along well together – but that Donne was not commonly irascible is shown by the fact that this is the one example recorded of his having actively quarrelled with anyone. Eventually, the argument was resolved: Alleyn made a settlement on Constance of two leases – of the Unicorn Inn at Southwark and of the Barge, Bell and Cock on Bankside (a well-known and popular brothel) – and gave security for the £1500 she was to receive at his death. He did in fact die only a short while afterwards, and his will left her a gift of £100 in cash in addition to the other bequests.

A letter written at this time to Sir Robert Carr, accompanying a poem Sir Robert had invited him to write, shows that Donne's mind was turning away from poetry (and indeed *An Hymn to the Saints* is probably the last poem he wrote). 'You know my uttermost when it was best', the Dean remarks, 'and even then I did best when I had least truth for my subjects. . . .' John Chamberlain, sending a copy of the verses to Sir Dudley Carleton, remarked: 'though they be reasonable witty and well done, yet I could wish a man of his years and place to give over versifying'. The attitude is astonishing to us, and indeed was not shared by all the readers who had come across Donne's poems in manuscript – on the other hand, for the majority his style was too allusive, too 'difficult' for immediate enjoyment; even Ben Jonson thought that Donne 'for not being understood, would perish'.

He did not commemorate in verse the event of 27 March 1625, which must have shaken him greatly: the death of the King. Though James had not been the kind of man naturally to endear himself to the clergy – 'he would make a great deal too bold with God', Sir Anthony Weldon recalled, 'both in cursing and swearing, and one strain higher verging on blasphemy. . . .' – Donne had always professed great gratitude to the King for leading him into the Church. On 3 April, he preached the first sermon Charles I heard on his accession.

Donne found the occasion a strain. The sermon was given at St James's Palace, where the Dean was unaccustomed to preach; he did not eat on the day of the sermon, and was obviously ill-at-ease. Charles left his private rooms for the first time since his father's death, Sir William Neve describing how he 'went after dinner into the chapel . . . Lord Danvers carrying the sword before him, his majesty looking

SPES MAGNA MINORIS ORBIS

BEHOLD GREAT BRITAINE THIS IS CHARLES THE FAIRE HIS BROTHERS PARTNER & HIS FATHERS HEIRE

London print. for

very pale, his visage being the true glass of his inward, as well as his accoutrements of external mourning'.

The Dean took as his text Psalm 11:3 – 'If the foundations be destroyed, what can the righteous do?' For the occasion, it was a rather over-intellectual sermon perhaps, though he spoke of the 'text of mortification' God had spread over England. A fortnight later, at Denmark House, where James's body was lying in state, he preached a more emotional sermon:

How poor, how faint, how pale, how momentary, how transitory, how empty, how frivolous, how dead things must you necessarily think titles and possessions and favours and all, when you see that hand which was the hand of destiny, of Christian destiny, of the Almighty God, lie dead? It was not so hard a hand when we touched it last, nor so cold a hand when we kissed it last. That hand which was wont to wipe all tears from all our eyes, doth now but press and squeeze us as so many sponges, filled one with one, another with another cause of tears – tears that can have no other bank to bound them but the declared and manifested will of God. For till our tears flow to that height that they might be called a murmuring against the declared will of God, it is against our allegiance, it is disloyalty, to give our tears any stop, any termination, any measure.

Later, dressed in heavy mourning and attended by one of his servants, the Dean of St Paul's walked behind the dead King in the funeral procession to Westminster Abbey.

In the early summer of 1625, Donne decided to move out to Chelsea for some fresh country air. He had been suffering from a troublesome cough – 'I had been long in my chamber, and practised how to put out breath, almost to my last gasp', he wrote to a friend. In June, he told his friend Sir Nicholas Carey that he had 'determined to remove myself and some few of my family to Chelsea, where I shall have room enough for so few, with conveniency, and so be near the business of our church, and not far removed from means of taking the liberty you have allowed me, to visit you sometimes'.

It was a very fortunate moment to choose to remove from the built-up area of the city, for London was soon in the grip of the worst outbreak of plague since the Black Death. While there had been for a century only two or three years during which no cases of plague at all had been reported, in August 1625 over three hundred people died in Donne's parish of St Dunstan's, where the normal death-rate would have been about twenty.

The Dean wrote vividly of the outbreak to Sir Thomas Roe, Ambassador at Constantinople:

Your number of 2000 [deaths] a day was so far attempted by us that in the city of London and in a mile compass, I believe there died 1000 a day. But by reason that these infections are not so frequent with us, the horror I pre-

(*Opposite*) Charles I. 'His exercises of religion were most exemplary, for every morning early, and evening not very late, singly and alone . . . he spent some time in private meditation. . . . And on Sundays and Tuesdays he came to the Chapel.'

Graphic illustrations to books and broadsheets convey the terror of the plague. 'The purple whip of vengeance, the plague, having beaten many thousands of men, women and children to death, and still marking the people of this city . . . is the only cause that all her inhabitants walk up and down like mourners at some great solemn funeral.'

sume was greater here, for the citizens fled away as out of a house on fire, and stuffed their pockets with their best ware, and threw themselves into the highways and were not received so much as into barns, and perished so, some of them with more money about them than would have bought the village where they died.

The city was almost empty. William Lilly, the astrologer, walked to church one morning and met only three people in the streets. Dekker reported how

all merry meetings are cut off, all frolic assemblies dissolved, and in their circles are raised up the black, sullen and dogged spirits of sadness, of melancholy. . . . Mirth is departed and lies dead and buried in men's bosoms; laughter dare not look a man in the face; jests are like music to the deaf, not regarded; pleasure itself finds now no pleasure but in sighing and bewailing the miseries of the time. . . . Playhouses stand like taverns that have cast out their masters, the doors are locked up, the flags, like their bushes, taken down – or rather like houses lately infected, from whence the affrighted dwellers are fled, in hope to live better in the country.

While members of Donne's congregations consulted astrologers and quacks to know whether they would live or die, or sought to assure their survival by drinking ale boiled with angelica and celandine, dragon-water and mithridate, by chewing dried angelica root or smelling the tasselled end of a ship's rope, or finally desperately tried to stave off death by plastering their plague-sores with newly killed pigeons cut in two, or a plaster of egg-yolk, honey and herb of grace, Donne naturally improved on the occasion with some of his finest sermons.

From the pulpit of St Dunstan's, he thundered against the poor victims,

cut off by the hand of God, some even in their robberies, in half-empty houses; and in their drunkenness in voluptuous and riotous houses; and in their lusts and wantonness in licentious houses; and so took in infection and death, like Judas' sop, death dipped and soaked in sin.

Men whose lust carried them into the jaws of infection in lewd houses, and seeking one sore perished with another; men whose rapine and covetousness broke into houses, and seeking the wardrobes of others, found their own winding-sheet, in the infection of that house where they stole their own death; men who sought no other way to divert sadness, but strong drink in riotous houses, and there drank up David's cup of Malediction, the cup of con-demned men, of death, in the infection of that place.

He looked clearly at the disaster, with eyes that seem almost over-keen, and certainly brought cold comfort to the parishioners he prompted to

consider upon what ground you tread: upon ground so holy, as that all the ground is made of the body of Christians, and therein hath received a second consecration. Every puff of wind within these walls may blow the father into the son's eye, or the wife into her husband's, or his into hers, or both into their children's, or their children's into both.

Every grain of dust that flies here, is a piece of a Christian. You need not dis-tinguish your pews by figures: you need not say, 'I sit within so many [inches] of such a neighbour,' but 'I sit within so many inches of my husband's, or wife's, or child's, or friend's grave.' Ambitious men never made more shift for places in court, than dead men for graves in churches; and as in our latter times we have seen two and two almost in every place and office, so almost every grave is oppressed with twins; and as at Christ's resurrection some of the dead arose out of their graves that were buried again, so in this lamentable calamity the dead were buried and thrown up again before they were resolved to dust, to make room for more.

The ground again was to be disturbed by such a burden in less than a generation, with the even greater epidemic of 1665. But this was bad enough.

Donne, his children and his fortunate servants lived during the plague in Sir John Danvers's house down by the river at Chelsea. His hostess, Lady Danvers, was an old, trusted and valued friend – formerly the Mrs Magdalen Herbert to whom he had addressed *The Autumnal* thirty years previously. Danvers himself was Member of

Parliament for Oxford University, and an intelligent and witty man. John Aubrey wrote:

He had well travelled in France and Italy and made good observations. He had in a fair body an harmonical mind. In his youth his complexion was so exceedingly beautiful and fine that Thomas Bond Esq., who was his companion in his travels, did say that the people would come after him in the street to admire him. He had a very fine fancy, which lay (chiefly) for gardens and architecture. The garden at Chelsea in Middlesex (as likewise the house there) do remain monuments of his ingenuity.

So one may picture Donne, though troubled by the epidemic and all its attendant horrors, nevertheless able to relax pleasantly in his host's Italian gardens, with their hedges, walks, flower-beds and Italianate carved figures.

He spent some of the time, at least, in revising and editing his sermons. In November, he wrote to Sir Thomas Roe: 'I have reviewed as many of my sermons as I had kept any notes of, and I have written out a great many, and hope to do more. I am already come to the number of eighty, of which my son, who I hope will take the same profession or some other in the world of middle understanding, may hereafter make some use.' It took Donne about eight hours to copy out one sermon; he worked hard during the five months he spent with the Danvers. There is a great contrast between his care over his theological writings, and his unconcern for his poems – especially the early, erotic ones still circulating in manuscript; the impression is that he would happily have recalled and perhaps even destroyed them if he had been able to do so.

The plague epidemic passed; Donne returned to the Deanery, and in February 1626 probably attended Charles's coronation at the Abbey. Then he became busy at the meetings in the Abbey of the Convocation of Canterbury, of which he was elected Prolocutor or Chairman. He made an extremely long and excessively convoluted Latin oration, and took charge of Convocation with a firm and businesslike hand. At the same time he continued to keep an eye on the parish of St Dunstan's, and to preach (his sermon before the King during Lent was commanded to be printed, and was dedicated to Charles). Now that the perils of plague were over, his mind turned to the more positive aspects of worship: he spoke of the delight of the Christian life, of hospitality and good company, of simple joy – 'Joy is peace for having done that which we ought to have done. . . . To have something to do, to do it, and then to rejoice in having done it; to embrace a calling, to perform the duties of that calling, to joy and rest in the peaceful testimony of having done so. This is Christianly done: Christ did it – angelically done: Angels do it – Godly done: God does it.'

Izaak Walton, angler and biographer; a man of gentle humour, wisdom and charity.

(*Below*) Izaak Walton's *Lives* of four seventeenth-century men was his first book; though sometimes inaccurate, it contains many first-hand anecdotes, and has great charm and immediacy.

It must have been during the 1620s that Donne first met Izaak Walton. Walton was keeping a linen-draper's shop in Fleet Street, and went to service at St Dunstan's. In 1626, Donne married him to Rachel Floud, and by that time it seems certain that the two men knew each other fairly well. Walton was not, at that time, a writer – indeed, his biography of Donne was the result of a simple, forthright admiration of the Dean rather than of an overpowering literary instinct. While there are errors of fact in it, it is still the best and fullest first-hand account of the poet and preacher's life, and the first real biography of an English poet.

At Christmas 1626, while the Dean's family was celebrating the festival, Lucy, his second daughter, only eighteen, suddenly died; she was buried on 9 January. In the Easter Sermon at St Paul's, he struck a deeply personal note:

If I had fixed a son in Court, or married a daughter into a plentiful fortune, I were satisfied for that son and that daughter. Shall I not be so when the King of Heaven hath taken that son to himself, and married himself to that daughter, for ever? . . . This is the faith that sustains me when I lose by the

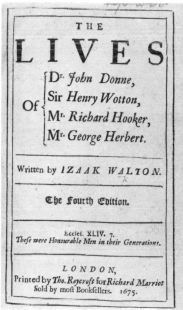

THE

LIVES

Of {
Dr. *John Donne*,
Sir *Henry Wotton*,
Mr. *Richard Hooker*,
Mr. *George Herbert*.
}

Written by *IZAAK WALTON*.

The Fourth Edition.

Ecclef. XLIV. 7.
These were Honourable Men in their Generations.

LONDON,
Printed by *Tho. Roycroft* for *Richard Marriot*
Sold by moft Bookfellers. 1675.

death of others, or when I suffer by living in misery myself: that the dead and we are now all in one Church, and at the resurrection shall be all in one choir.

Death was coming, too, for Donne's older friends. Sir Henry Goodyer died in March 1627; then, in May and June, Lady Bedford and Lady Danvers, the first now a somewhat shadowy figure, outside Donne's circle, but the latter still a dear friend, also died. Donne, who only two years before had been Lady Danvers's guest at Chelsea, preached a commemorative sermon to a congregation of friends. Walton was there, and heard the sermon, which like so many of Donne's sermons on death brought the vividness of his belief in the resurrection to the comfort of the mourners:

That body upon which you tread now, that body which now while I speak is mouldering and crumbling into less and less dust, and so hath some motion, though no life; that body . . . that was eyes to the blind and hands and feet to the lame while it lived, and being dead is so still by having been so lively an example to teach others to be so; that body at last shall have her last expectation satisfied, and dwell bodily with that righteousness, in these new heavens and new earth, for ever and ever and ever, and infinite and super-infinite evers.

During April, Donne inadvertently upset King Charles by a tactless reference to the Queen in a Court sermon. He had to beg pardon, and though he was readily forgiven, there was a hint that his position

Charles I, with Queen Henrietta Maria and their children.

might not perhaps be as secure as it had been under the old King. He was not so disturbed, however, that he was unable to continue with his normal busy life as ecclesiastical administrator, and he continued to preach as regularly as ever.

In February 1627, another good friend, Christopher Brooke (who had given away the bride at Donne's wedding) died, leaving 'my picture of Mary Magdalene, and my night shadowed picture, and piece of Apollo and the Muses – being an original of an Italian Master's hand (as I have been made believe)' to 'my dear ancient and worthy friend Dr Donne, the dean of Paul's'. (It is worth noting, by the way, that in the original will, as in other contemporary documents, Donne's name is spelt *Dunn*, which gives us a sufficient clue to its proper pronunciation.)

He had still his children, of course; but Con's marriage had been at best only an indifferent success, and his two sons were from home. John, the elder, had left Westminster School in 1622 and gone to Christ Church, Oxford; he may have been married, briefly, in 1627; and while his father hoped to see him in Holy Orders, it is possible that he may not have become a clergyman until after the Dean's death. George, the second son, was a soldier who by 1627 had served as Sergeant-Major under Buckingham against the French. Bridget was still at home, and so were Margaret and Elizabeth, but they were still too young to give their father much really intimate friendship or comfort. In a letter, he had written an acquaintance that 'when I lend the world a daughter in marriage, or lend the world a son in a profession, the world does not always pay me well again; my hopes are not always answered in that daughter or that son' – which is perhaps a hint that family relationships were somewhat strained.

Donne was not yet an old man, in our terms – only fifty-six; but he was not strong. In the summer of 1627 he had had a bad attack of tonsilitis, and the doctors had bled and starved him, weakening his constitution still further. 'I should be sorry if this should make me a silenced Minister', he had written wryly. In fact, carefully nursing his throat, he made a more or less complete recovery from the tonsilitis, and was able to go on preaching as regularly as ever. Then, in June 1630, came a pleasant interlude: he travelled out to Camberwell to attend the wedding of his widowed daughter Con to Samuel Harvey. Two months later, he visited the couple, and at their home went down with a fever.

From his correspondence, we gather that for some time he had been fighting recurring fevers. This one was worse than usual, and he was forced to decline the usual invitation to preach before the King early in November. 'I am afraid I shall not recover confidence to come to London till the spring be a little advanced', he wrote to a friend, and arranged for a substitute to preach in St Paul's at Christmas.

George Villiers, the first Duke of Buckingham. 'How to use a sword, when it is out, we know you know. Think you that commandment of our Saviour's to be directed upon you, "Put up the sword; study the ways of peace."'

The news of his illness became public, and there were rumours that he had died. 'A man would almost be content to die (if there were no other benefit in death) to hear of so much sorrow and so much good testimony from good men as I (God be blessed for it) did upon the report of my death', he wrote.

The extent of the rumours showed how well known Donne had become during recent years – both as Dean and poet. A Dutchman, Constantine Huygens, was visiting England in 1630, and wrote home:

'In poetry Donne is more famous than anyone. Many rich fruits from the green branches of his wit have lain mellowing among the lovers of art, which now, when nearly rotted with age, they are distributing. Into my hands have fallen . . . some twenty-five of the best sort.' A poet himself, Huygens had translated the manuscript verses into Dutch.

Donne struggled back to London early in February 1631, though racked with toothache, troubled by a sore throat, afflicted with deafness, and weak from his fevers. He had barely arrived back at the Deanery when his old mother died; she was buried on 28 January, and her death may have been the shock which prevented him carrying out his intention of preaching on Candlemas Day (2 February). He still intended to preach before the King at Whitehall on the first Friday in Lent – 12 February – despite increasing weakness. He attempted to build up his strength by taking various 'cordials', and even by drinking quantities of milk, which he hated, but which was pressed upon him by his friend Dr Fox. Finally, he rebelled: he would not, he said, 'drink it ten days longer upon the best moral assurance of having twenty years added to his life'.

He mounted the pulpit in the chapel at Whitehall as though he were already a dead man. Walton leaves an unforgettable description of the occasion:

At his coming thither, many of his friends – who with sorrow saw his sickness had left him but so much flesh as did only cover his bones – doubted his strength to perform that task, and did therefore dissuade him from undertaking it, assuring him, however, it was like to shorten his life. But he passionately denied their requests, saying 'he could not doubt that that God who in so many weaknesses had assisted him with an unexpected strength, would now withdraw it in his last employment; professing an holy ambition to perform that sacred work.' And when, to the amazement of some beholders, he appeared in the pulpit, many of them thought he presented himself not to preach mortification by a living voice, but mortality by a decayed body and a dying face. And doubtless many did secretly ask that question in Ezekiel: 'Do these bones live?'

In his last sermon, Donne faced his impending death with steady resolution. Death was not then looked upon as the obscenity it has become in the twentieth century: not only was it constantly before seventeenth-century man (so many of Donne's children died young; so many of his contemporaries were stricken down in the prime of life by the plague, or some other then fatal sickness) but there was absolute belief in the resurrection and eternal life. The Dean's last sermon was later entitled *Death's Duel, or, a Consolation to the Soul against the dying Life and living Death of the Body*. Man walked with death throughout his life, he told his congregation; and death was not an unworthy companion.

We have a winding sheet in our mother's womb, which grows with us from our conception, and we come into the world wound up in that winding sheet, for we come to seek a grave. . . . We celebrate our own funeral with cries, even at our birth . . . we come into a world that lasts many ages, but we last not. . . .

This whole world is but an universal churchyard, but our common grave, and the life and motion that the greatest persons have in it, is but as the shaking of buried bodies in their grave, by an earthquake. . . .

That all that monarch who spread over many nations alive, must in his dust lie in a corner of that sheet of lead, and there, but so long as that lead will last; and that private and retired man that thought himself his own for ever, and never came forth, must in his dust of the grave be published and (such are the revolutions of the graves) be mingled with the dust of every highway, and of every dunghill, and swallowed in every puddle and pond; this is the most inglorious and contemptible vilification, the most deadly and peremptory nullification of man that we can consider.

The words, coming from a man standing so obviously at the edge of his own grave, must have been chilling. But he offered them, of course, not as evidence of the worthlessness of man's life, but of the glory of it through the intervention of God's mercy. That he himself had come to terms with his own fate, is seen in an extraordinary conversation recorded by Walton. Donne met a friend, the day after his last sermon had been delivered; the friend taxed him with having preached a depressed and depressing sermon. Not so, Donne rejoined:

I was in a serious contemplation of the providence and goodness of God to me . . . and looking back on my life past, I now plainly see it was his hand that prevented me from all temporal employment; and that it was his will I should never settle nor thrive till I entered into the ministry, in which I have now lived almost twenty years (I hope to his glory), and by which I most humbly thank him I have been enabled to requite most of those friends which showed me kindness when my fortune was very low, as God knows it was. . . . I have lived to be useful and comfortable to my good father-in-law Sir George More . . . I have maintained my own mother, whom it hath pleased God after a plentiful fortune in her younger days to bring to a great decay in her very old age. . . .

I cannot plead innocency of life, especially of my youth; but I am to be judged by a merciful God . . . and though of myself I have nothing to present to him but sins and misery, yet I know he looks not upon me now as I am of myself, but as I am in my saviour, and he hath given me even at this present time some testimonies by his Holy Spirit, that I am of the number of his elect. I am therefore full of unexpressible joy, and shall die in peace.

Donne's last days were dominated entirely by his preparations for death. His will had already been made, written in his own lawyer's hand, disposing of his collection of paintings, of the souvenirs of his life (such as the Dort medal), making gifts to his servants – coachman,

The engraving of Donne in his
shroud used as a frontispiece for
Death's Duell, 1632, and *(opposite)*
his effigy by Nicholas Stone, in St
Paul's Cathedral. *One short sleep
past, we wake eternally, | And death
shall be no more. Death, thou shalt die.*

boy, maids – to the poor of St Dunstan's, to some of his colleagues at
St Paul's, and of course to his children.

Now, there was the question of a memorial to be set over the grave
that was to be prepared for him, at his own request, in St Paul's. A
large wooden urn was carved in wood, and, leaving his sick-bed,
Donne stripped off his clothes and was dressed in his shroud, knotted
at the head and the foot; then he stood on the urn, eyes closed, while an
artist made a life-size sketch. From this, Nicholas Stone later carved
the stone figure which was to become perhaps the most famous monument of the period, and which, miraculously surviving the Great
Fire thirty years later, still stands in the Cathedral.

The sketch finished, Donne retired to bed, and there said farewell
to his friends. On 31 March 1631, he died: 'as his soul ascended and his

last breath departed from him', Walton wrote, 'he closed his own eyes, and then disposed his hands and body into such a posture as required not the least alteration by those that came to shroud him.'

He had asked in his will to be buried 'in the most private manner that may be'; but privacy was impossible. There was a very large attendance at the funeral, including John Donne the younger, but not George, who was in Cadiz, a prisoner of the Spaniards. The coffin was lowered into the grave dug in the south aisle of the Cathedral, behind the choir. Then, Walton says,

to the place of his burial some mournful friends repaired, and . . . strewed his [grave] with an abundance of curious and costly flowers; which course they, who were never yet known, continued morning and evening for many days, not ceasing till the stones that were taken up in the Church, to give his body admission into the cold earth – now his bed of rest – were again by the mason's art so levelled and firmed as they had been formerly, and his place of burial indistinguishable to common view. The next day after his burial, some un-known friend, some one of the many lovers and admirers of his virtue and learning, writ this epitaph with a coal on the wall over his grave:

> Reader! I am to let thee know
> Donne's body only lies below;
> For, could the grave his soul comprise,
> Earth would be richer than the skies.

At his death, Donne's reputation as a preacher was high not only with the congregation at St Paul's and St Dunstan's, but more widely. His reputation as a poet rested on manuscript copies of his verses (only seven of his poems, and part of one more, had been printed during his lifetime). Between 1633 and 1669, there were to be seven printed editions of his poetry, and his son John was to publish some of the sermons. But it was not until the twentieth century that his full glory as a poet was to be widely recognized.

The quality of his prose has never been in question, when it has been read at all. Coleridge's assertion that 'he was an orthodox christian only because he could have been an infidel more easily; and therefore willed to be a christian', in part accounts for the denigra-tion of the sermons *as theology* by a number of critics who (like T. S. Eliot) had the highest regard for him as a writer. His prose was scarcely bettered in his time.

Contemporary poets had been among the relatively small number of readers who had sought out Donne's poems in manuscript long before the first collection was printed in 1633. They were influenced by the poems' intensely speculative nature, which led Dr Johnson to coin the phrase 'metaphysical poets' to describe those who took roughly the same path. 'If their conceits were far-fetched they were often worth the carriage', he pointed out.

The difficulties which stood between the reader and an immediate enjoyment of Donne's poetry (and in part the poetry of, say, John Marston, George Turberville or Barnabe Googe) included the 'intolerably harsh and crabbed versification', as the Victorian critic Edmund Gosse was to put it. But Donne also referred constantly to elements of 'the new philosophy' and to new scientific theories with which most Jacobeans would have been unfamiliar. Many of his readers must have regarded his poetry with much the same sense of bewilderment as the common reader coming to Eliot's *The Waste Land* in 1922 (Eliot's own debt to Donne was, of course, considerable).

For two centuries, then, the *poet* Donne was neglected. Then, in the late nineteenth century, a revaluation began. Browning, Rossetti, Swinburne read and admired him; others followed. There are still some difficulties: though many of the scientific references are now part of our common knowledge, the style is still uncommon enough to perplex. Neither can Donne be read for pastime, as some of his contemporaries may (George Herbert, the best of the metaphysicals after him, may use surprising and original imagery, but is much more consciously 'poetic' – full of melody). With Donne one is forced to pay attention, in part by the ever-changing rhythm; this is not verse for the inattentive 'poetry-lover' content to float with a tide of smooth prosody. One must fight the rough lines to subdue them and see through to their bare bones.

But the fight is not, after all, too difficult. One of the most revelatory of all exercises is to read Donne aloud: when one does so, the cunning of emphases and the breaking-up of the rhythms disclose his meaning. There is the most profound *over-all* rhythmic pattern to a poem such as *The sun rising*: the effect is almost that of a screenplay – highly visual in imagery, broken up into separate 'shots', but edited into a wonderfully coherent whole. It was Coleridge who said that 'to read Donne you must measure Time, and discover the Time of each word by the sense of Passion'.

Donne worked when classicism was giving way to a new movement, yet giving way reluctantly, so that its influence was still felt in the 'new' verse of Ben Jonson, Michael Drayton, Samuel Daniel. Others tore themselves away from this classical influence – they were on the side of experiment, and they were radicals who were also social critics. Donne was of this company, like Yeats in seeking to reveal in nakedness 'the foul rag-and-bone-shop of the heart'.

The *Satires* are obvious examples of his pioneering spirit as far as social criticism goes. But in the love poems one finds a radical moral tone illuminated by experiments in prosody and form, by images which would never have occurred to any poet before him as being possible, and which perhaps only in our own time have seemed natural and have had their full effect.

Donne looks at life through his poetry in a manner which Eliot and Pound made familiar to us in the 1920s. He seems to us, now, a modern – not only technically, but because his attitudes are nearer our own than those of any other poet of his age. One of the few great reformers and preservers of the English tongue, as Eliot called him, and the writer of the greatest love poems in the language, he has at last put on immortality and will never again be seen without the singing-robes which he made new for his time, and which remain fresh and original for ours.

1572 born in Bread Street, London, between 24 January and 19 June

1576 death of father

1584 matriculates from Hart Hall, Oxford

1588 probably at Cambridge

1589 probably travels abroad

1592 enters Lincoln's Inn

1593 brother Henry dies in Newgate Prison

1596 sails on the Cadiz expedition

1597 sails on the 'Islands' expedition; writing his early poems. Becomes secretary to Lord Keeper Egerton

1601 MP for Brackley. At the turn of the year, secretly marries Ann More

1602 reveals his marriage; dismissed and imprisoned. Finds refuge at Pyrford

1603 daughter Constance born

1604 son John born

1605 travels with Sir Walter Chute in Europe; son George born

1606 returns to England; settles at Mitcham

1607 son Francis born

1608 daughter Lucy born

1609 daughter Bridget born

1610 publishes *Pseudo-Martyr*

1611 daughter Mary born. Depression at inactivity relieved by meetings with friends in London. To France with Sir Robert Drury

1612 with the Druries to Germany and Belgium. In London, taken a house in Drury Lane

1613 son Nicholas born, but dies in infancy. The family falls ill

1614 MP for Taunton in disreputable Parliament. Daughter Mary dies. Son Francis dies

1615 ordained, January. Appointed a royal Chaplain to James I. Daughter Margaret born

1616 Rector of Keyston. Preaches at Court. Daughter Elizabeth born. Rector of Sevenoaks. Divinity reader at Lincoln's Inn

1617 wife Ann dies after giving birth to stillborn child, 15 August

1619 chaplain to Viscount Doncaster's embassage to Germany

1621 Dean of St Paul's, 22 November

1622 Rector of Blunham. JP

1623 arranges marriage of Constance to Edward Alleyn. Seriously ill

1624 Vicar of St Dunstan's-in-the West

1625 preaches first sermon before Charles I. Quarrels with Alleyn. Preaches on the plague; retires to Chelsea

1626 death of daughter Lucy at Christmas

1627 distressed by death of friends

1630 falls seriously ill in autumn

1631 mother dies, 28 January. Donne dies, 31 March; buried in St Paul's, 3 April

1633 first edition of *Collected Poems*

1640 publication of *Eighty Sermons*

1649 *Fifty Sermons*

1651 Selected *Letters*; *Essays in Divinity*

1661 *Twenty-Six Sermons*

SOURCES AND BIBLIOGRAPHY

Many attempts have been made to prepare a wholly satisfactory edition of Donne's poems. The most accessible, and one of the best, is that edited for Penguin Education by A. J. Smith: entitled the *Complete English Poems*, it was published by Penguin Books in 1971, and is the source I have used when quoting from the poems. *The Sermons of John Donne* were edited in ten lengthy volumes by G. R. Potter and Evelyn M. Simpson, and published by the University of California Press (1953–62). I have used that edition as the source for quotations from the sermons, but have modernized the spelling (as I have done in quotations from the poems); in the prose, where it has seemed desirable for the sake of clarity and easy readability, I have modernized the punctuation also, as I have done in quoting from Izaak Walton and other contemporaries. The general reader looking for a useful anthology of Donne's sermons can go to *Donne's Sermons*, prepared in 1919 by Logan Pearsall Smith, and still available from Oxford University Press. OUP also publishes Helen Gardner's 1967 anthology of *Selected Prose*, which includes, as well as extracts from some sermons, passages from the *Paradoxes* and *Problems*, *Biathanatos*, *Pseudo-Martyr* and other works.

Unless new material unexpectedly appears (from, perhaps, the libraries of some of the continental universities in the cities Donne visited on his travels in Europe) it is difficult to believe that a fuller biography will ever be written than R. C. Bald's *John Donne: a Life*, published by Oxford University Press in 1970. Every available fact is reported there, and the conjectures are well argued.

From the great body of work about Donne, the following can be recommended:

A. Alvarez, *The School of Donne* (London 1961)

J. B. Leishman, *Donne, the Monarch of Wit* (London 1962)

E. M. Simpson, *A Study of the Prose Works of John Donne* (Oxford 1948)

Theodore Spencer (ed.), *A Garland for John Donne* (New York 1932)

L. Unger, *Donne's Poetry and Modern Criticism* (Chicago 1962)

Izaak Walton, *Life of Donne* ed. George Saintsbury (Oxford 1927)

LIST OF ILLUSTRATIONS

The details in square brackets refer to the derivation of caption quotations, which are from Donne unless otherwise stated.

Frontispiece: Portrait of John Donne. Oil painting by an unknown artist, *c.* 1595. *Collection the Marquis of Lothian. Photo National Portrait Gallery, London.*

5 Ralph Aggas's *View of London, c.* 1560–70. Published by the London Topographical Society, December 1905. *British Library.*

6 Portrait of John Heywood. Woodcut from *John Heywoodes woorkes,* 1562. *British Library. Photo Raymond Mander and Joe Mitchenson Theatre Collection.*

7 John Donne Sr's name recorded in the Freedom Book of the Ironmonger's Company. *By kind permission of the Worshipful Company of Ironmongers. Photo Eileen Tweedy.*

8 Lord Mayor in procession. Early seventeenth-century manuscript illumination. *British Library,* Add. MS. 16889 fol. 22.

9 'A Thankfull Remembrance of God's Mercie'. Broadsheet, representing Popish plots and treasons from the beginning of the reign of Queen Elizabeth I, 1569. *Courtesy of the Trustees of the British Museum.*

10 Oxford. Engraving from Braun and Hohenberg's *Civitas Orbis Terrarum,* 1573–1618. *British Library.*

11 Portrait of Sir Henry Wotton (1568–1639). Canvas by an unknown artist. *National Portrait Gallery, London.*

12 Cambridge. Engraving from Braun and Hohenberg's *Civitas Orbis Terrarum,* 1573–1618. *British Library.*

13 Travelling coach. Engraving by John Dunstall, seventeenth century. *London Prospects Portfolio,* Vol. V. *Society of Antiquaries, London.*

15 Nos. 16–19 Old Buildings, Lincoln's Inn, from the north. Built in the sixteenth century. *Photo Country Life.* [*Satire I,* 11 2/4.]

16 Verse-letter from John Donne to Lady Carey and Mistress Essex Rich, 1612. *Bodleian Library, Oxford,* MS. Eng. Poet d. 197^r. Lady Carey and Mistress Essex Rich were sisters, whom Donne probably never met. Their brother, Sir Robert Rich, may have met Donne in Amiens (where he was staying) and suggested that he should write something in praise of his

sisters. The MS. was discovered in 1970.

17 Woodcut from the songsheet 'An Answer to Moggy's Misfortune'. From Vol. 2 of the *Roxburghe Ballads*, late sixteenth–early seventeenth century. *British Library*. [*Elegy III*, *ll 11/13*.]

19 Portrait of John Donne. Engraving by William Marshall, 1591. *British Library*. Both Lawrence Binyon and John Bryson (who discovered the portrait which forms the frontispiece of this book) believed the Marshall engraving to be taken from a lost Hilliard miniature. ['The Storm', *ll 3/5*.]

22 The Earl of Essex. Engraving by T. Cockson (1591–1636). *Courtesy of the Trustees of the British Museum.*

23 The Armada Portrait of Elizabeth I. Canvas by Marcus Gheeraerts (*c.* 1590–1625). *From the Woburn Abbey Collection, by kind permission of His Grace, the Duke of Bedford.*

John Donne's seal. Salisbury Cathedral library. *Photo Anthony Miles Ltd.*

24 Portrait of Sir Walter Raleigh (*c.* 1552–1618). Panel attributed to the monogrammist 'H', 1588. *National Portrait Gallery, London.* [John Aubrey, *Brief Lives.*]

25 The Battle of Cadiz, 1596. Contemporary engraving.

National Maritime Museum, London.

27 Portrait of Sir Thomas Egerton (*c.* 1540–1617). Panel by an unknown artist. *National Portrait Gallery, London.* [Izaak Walton, *Life of Donne.*]

28 The Courts of King's Bench and Chancery in Westminster Hall. Pen and brown ink with brown wash by an anonymous draughtsman, possibly Dutch. Mid-seventeenth century. *Courtesy of the Trustees of the British Museum.*

29 Whitehall Palace and great houses bordering the river. Engraving from C. J. Visscher's *View of London*, *c.* 1616. *Courtesy of the Trustees of the British Museum.*

Drawing of Whitehall Stairs and part of Whitehall Palace; late sixteenth–early seventeenth century. *Ashmolean Museum, Oxford.*

York House by the Thames. Detail from the *Panorama of Elizabethan London* drawn by Anthony van den Wyngaerde. *Ashmolean Museum, Oxford.*

31 Portrait of Sir George More (1553–1632). Panel. British School. *Private Collection. Photo Courtauld Institute of Art, University of London.* [Sir John Oglander, *A Royalist's Notebook.*]

North front of Loseley Park, built 1561–69. *Photo Gale and Polden Ltd, Aldershot.*

32 Nonsuch House. Drawing by G. Hoefnagel, 1560. *Courtesy of the Trustees of the British Museum.* [George Braun, *Urbium Praecipuarum Mundi Theatrum Quintum*, 1582.]

34 Sir George More's bedroom, Loseley Park. *Photo English Life Publications Ltd, Derby.*

35 The drawing-room, Loseley Park. *Photo English Life Publications Ltd, Derby.*

36 Letter from John Donne to Sir Robert Cotton, 20 February 1602. *British Library*, Cotton MS. Julius C. iii fol. 153.

37 Receipt from John Donne, in his own hand, to Sir Thomas Egerton, 6 July 1602. *By permission of the Folger Shakespeare Library, Washington DC.*

38 Detail of John Norden's map of Surrey, 1610. *British Library.*

40 Head of the funeral procession of Elizabeth I. Early seventeenth-century manuscript illumination. *British Library*, Add. MS. 35324 fol. 31v. [*A Sermon preached at Paul's Cross . . .* , 24 March 1616.]

Paris. Engraving from Braun and Hohenberg's *Civitas Orbis Terrarum*, 1573–1618. *British Library.*

42 John Donne's scribe's copy of *Biathanatos*, inscribed in Donne's own hand to Sir Edward Herbert. *Bodleian Library, Oxford*, MS. e. Mus. 131 fol. IX$^\text{v}$.

43 John Donne's house at Mitcham. Woodcut after a sketch by Richard Simpson, later the biographer of the Jesuit theologian Edmund Campion; Simpson lived in Donne's house as a child. From Augustus Jessop's *John Donne*, 1897. *British Library.*

44 Lucy Harrington, Countess of Bedford (1581–1627). Miniature by Isaac Oliver, *c.* 1605. *Fitzwilliam Museum, Cambridge.*

45 Portrait of Lucy Harrington, Countess of Bedford (1581–1627). Oil painting by William Larkin. *Gripsholm Castle, Sweden. Photo Svenska Porträttarkivet Nationalmuseum, Stockholm.* [*To the Countess of Bedford: Madam/You have refined me*, 11 55/60.]

46 Elizabeth Stanley, Countess of Huntingdon. Engraving by William Marshall, *c.* 1617–33. *Courtesy of the Trustees of the British Museum.* [*To the Countess of Huntingdon: Madam/Man to God's image . . .* , 11 15/16.]

Map of Westminster. From John Norden's *Speculum Britanniae*, 1593. *British Library.*

47 Portrait of Edward Herbert of Cherbury (1583–1648). Canvas, perhaps after Isaac Oliver. *National Portrait Gallery, London.* [*To Sir Edward Herbert, at Juliers*, 11 49/50.]

48 *The Powder Treason.* Broadsheet engraved by M. Droeshout, 1605. *Courtesy of the Trustees of the British Museum.*

49 The Gunpowder Plot: the execution of Guy Fawkes and other conspirators. Drawing by C. J. Visscher, early seventeenth century. *Courtesy of the Trustees of the British Museum.*

50 '. . . the true portraiture of the Jesuits and priests: as they use to sitt at Counsell in England to further ye Catholicke Cause.' Broadsheet, 1620. *Courtesy of the Trustees of the British Museum.* [Parliament's Petition of 3 December 1621 to James I.]

52 Titlepage to Thomas Coryate's *Crudities*, 1611. *British Library.* [*Upon Mr. Coryat's Crudities,* 11 75/6.]

53 Portrait of Ben Jonson (*c.* 1573–1637). Painting after A. Blyenberch. *National Portrait Gallery, London.* [Ben Jonson, *Epigram 23.*]

54 'Tittle-Tattle; or, the Several Branches of Gossipping'. Broadsheet, 1603. *Courtesy of the Trustees of the British Museum.*

Street-sellers. From the *Cries of the City of London*, seventeenth century. *Courtesy of the Trustees of the British Museum.* [Frederick, Duke of Würtemburg.]

57 Louis XIII and Anne of Austria. Engraving by P. Firens, early seventeenth century. *Courtesy of the Trustees of the British Museum.*

58 The 'Carrousel' given at the Place Royale on 5, 6, 7 April 1612, on the occasion of peace with the Spanish and news of the Spanish marriage. Engraving by Polon. *Bibliothèque Nationale, Paris.* [Letter to Sir Henry Goodyer.]

60 Aachen. Woodcut from Ludovico Guicciardini's *Description de touts les Pays-Bas*, 1613. *British Library.*

61 Map showing Lincoln's Inn Fields, Drury Lane and the Strand. Engraved by Wenceslaus Hollar, *c.* 1636. *Courtesy of the Trustees of the British Museum.* [Indenture of Sir Robert Drury's property, 1615.]

62 Portrait of Sir Robert Ker, Earl of Somerset (*c.* 1587–1645). Panel after J. Hoskins, *c.* 1620–25. *National Portrait Gallery, London.*

Portrait of James Hay, Viscount Doncaster (d. 1636). Engraving by Simon Passeus. *Courtesy of the Trustees of the British Museum.*

63 The Earl and Countess of Somerset. Engraving by Renold Elstrack, *c.* 1600–25. *Courtesy of the Trustees of the British Museum.* [*Eclogue and Epithalamion,* 1613, 11 223/5.)

The Tower of London. Etching by Wenceslaus Hollar, *c.* 1636. *Courtesy of the Trustees of the British Museum.*

65 James I in Parliament. Engraving by Renold Elstrack, *c.* 1603–25. *Courtesy of the*

1603–21. *Reproduced by gracious permission of Her Majesty the Queen.* [Sir Anthony Weldon, *Court and Character of James I,* 1650.]

84 The nave, Old St Paul's. Engraving by Wenceslaus Hollar, 1652. *Courtesy of the Trustees of the British Museum.*

85 Portrait of John Donne. Oil painting by an unknown artist, 1620. The Deanery, St Paul's Cathedral. *By courtesy of the Dean of St Paul's.*

86 Old St Paul's and Bow Church. Detail of engraving from C. J. Visscher's *View of London, c.* 1616. *Courtesy of the Trustees of the British Museum.*

88 Titlepage to *LXXX Sermons.* Engraved by Matthaus Merian II, 1640. *Courtesy of the Trustees of the British Museum.*

89 Interior looking west of the Church of St Edmund, Blunham, Bedfordshire. *Photo National Monuments Record.*

Inscription on the base of the silver chalice presented by John Donne to Blunham Church. *Photo National Monuments Record.*

93 Portrait of Edward Alleyn (1566–1626). Canvas by an unknown artist. *By permission of the Governors of Dulwich College Picture Library.*

94 Titlepage to *Five Sermons upon Speciall Occasions,* 1626. The British Library.

98 Charles I before his accession to the throne. Engraving by William Hole, *c.* 1609–24. *Courtesy of the Trustees of the British Museum.* [Sir Philip Warwick, *Memoirs of the Reign of Charles I.*]

100 Titlepage to Thomas Dekker's *A Rod for Runaways,* 1625. *British Library.* [Thomas Dekker, *Works for Armourers,* 1609.]

103 Portrait of Izaak Walton. Canvas by J. Huysmans, *c.* 1675. *National Portrait Gallery, London.*

Titlepage to Izaak Walton's *The Lives,* 1675. *British Library.*

104 Charles I, Henrietta Maria and their children. Engraving by William Marshall, *c.* 1630. *Courtesy of the Trustees of the British Museum.*

107 Portrait of George Villiers, 1st Duke of Buckingham (1592–1628). Canvas by an unknown artist. *National Portrait Gallery, London.* [Letter to the Duke of Buckingham, 1623.]

110 John Donne in his shroud. Frontispiece engraving for *Death's Duell,* 1632. *British Library.*

111 John Donne's effigy by Nicholas Stone, 1631. St Paul's Cathedral, south aisle. *Photo National Monuments Record.* [*Divine Meditations,* 10: *Death be not proud,* 11 13/14.]

INDEX

Page numbers in italics indicate illustrations; the number is not repeated where there are text references, as well as an illustration, on the same page.